T0205962

Lecture Notes in Computer Science 13417

More information about this series at https://link.springer.com/bookseries/558

Charalampos Saitis · Ildar Farkhatdinov ·
Stefano Papetti (Eds.)

Haptic and Audio Interaction Design

11th International Workshop, HAID 2022
London, UK, August 25–26, 2022
Proceedings

 Springer

Editors
Charalampos Saitis (iD)
Queen Mary University of London
London, UK

Ildar Farkhatdinov (iD)
Queen Mary University of London
London, UK

Stefano Papetti (iD)
Zürcher Hochschule der Künste
Zürich, Zürich, Switzerland

ISSN 0302-9743   ISSN 1611-3349 (electronic)
Lecture Notes in Computer Science
ISBN 978-3-031-15018-0   ISBN 978-3-031-15019-7 (eBook)
https://doi.org/10.1007/978-3-031-15019-7

This Springer imprint is published by the registered company Springer Nature Switzerland AG
The registered company address is: Gewerbestrasse 11, 6330 Cham, Switzerland

Preface

Since its conception by Stephen Brewster in 2006, the aim of the International Workshop on Haptic and Audio Interaction Design (HAID) is to bring together researchers and practitioners who share an interest in finding out how the haptic and audio modalities can be used in human-computer/machine interaction. The research challenges in the area are best approached through user-centered design, empirical studies, or the development of novel theoretical frameworks. To promote this research direction, HAID workshops were held every year between 2006 and 2013 (Glasgow, Seoul, Jyväskylä, Dresden, Copenhagen, Kyoto, Lund, Daejeon) with proceedings published as part of the Springer LNCS series, then discontinued.

During a six year hiatus the community remained active, with a focus on what came to be termed *"musical haptics"*. In February 2016, Stefano Papetti hosted the workshop "Haptics and Musical Practice: From audio-tactile psychophysics to the design and evaluation of digital musical interfaces" at the Zurich University of the Arts (Switzerland), and shortly after he organized a related workshop "Musical Haptics: Use and relevance of haptic feedback in musical practice" during the EuroHaptics 2016 conference in London, UK. These two workshops led to the open access volume Musical Haptics (Springer, 2018), edited by Stefano Papetti and Charalampos Saitis, the first ever scientific collection on the subject of haptics and audio-haptic interaction in music performance and perception.

Meanwhile, in December 2016, a symposium on "Force-Feedback and Music" was organized by Marcelo Wanderley at McGill University (Montreal, Canada), an institution with a long tradition in musical haptics research. Thomas Pietrzak and Marcelo Wanderley subsequently initiated an effort to revive the HAID community with new workshops in 2019 (Lille, France) and 2020 (Montreal, Canada; held online due to the COVID-19 pandemic), including self-published online proceedings and a related special issue of the Journal of Multimodal User Interfaces (Springer, 2020).

HAID 2022 was the 11th edition of the workshop, held during August 25–26, 2022, in London, UK. It was organized by the Centre for Digital Music and the Centre for Advanced Robotics at Queen Mary University of London, two established research groups hosting a critical mass of academics, researchers, and students investigating topics and methods relevant to HAID. As organizers and program chairs, we put emphasis on growing the community further, but also in a more sustainable way, engaging for the first time key scientific stakeholders (the IEEE Technical Committee on Haptics, the EuroHaptics Society, and the Audio Engineering Society) and an advisory board of international experts. A "Work in Progress" initiative was also introduced to increase inclusiveness of the community by helping HAID newcomers, especially underrepresented groups, to position their work within the HAID debate.

Despite challenges posed by the ongoing COVID-19 pandemic, both in terms of conducting haptics-based research and resuming international travel, HAID 2022 received a total of 19 full paper submissions, a more than twofold increase from the 2019 and 2020 editions. Each paper was peer-assessed by at least two reviewers and one meta-reviewer, using a pool of distinguished international experts, to whom we are grateful for the quality of their reviews, time and patience. In the end, 13 full papers were accepted and organized into four thematic sections, which are briefly introduced below.

Accessibility. Haptic and audio interaction brings most important benefits in situations where having access to and understanding speech and/or music may be hindered by a hearing impairment. Paté et al. presented a portable device that transforms music signals into symbolic vibrations, co-designed with stakeholders from the deaf and hard of hearing community to promote more inclusive live concert experiences. A plug-and-play audio-to-haptic feedback cover for smartphones was introduced by Ganis et al., who showed that normal hearing participants using cochlear implant simulation identified melodic contours better with than without haptic cues. Reed et al. shared evidence of improved lipreading when phonemic-based tactile signals are presented alongside a visual display.

Perception. Understanding haptic perception is key to designing effective multisensory displays. When they added a subthreshold vibrotactile stimulus to an electrotactile display, Balasubramanian et al. found that tactile masking was rendered absent and the perceived intensity of the display was increased. Jones and Ho reviewed psychophysical studies revealing temporal and spatial differences between the perception of cold and warm stimuli, and between those and tactile signals, in the context of thermo-haptic interaction design. Another set of perceptual experiments discussed by Paisa et al. demonstrated that different areas of the hand are variably sensitive to different vibration frequencies. Consigny et al. introduced a concept of perceptual total harmonic distortion for quantized tactile signals, which they used to demonstrate that 8-bit quantization can be imperceptible.

Design and Applications. Research in designing haptic-audio interaction for multisensory experiences has grown in recent years. Richards et al. reflected on the cross-influence between speculative design (research) and product design (industry) processes that led to the prototyping and realization of a wearable audio-tactile device for augmented listening. Soave et al. examined sound design aspects for the perception of motion in multisensory virtual reality environments. Brown and Farkhatdinov applied particle jamming to design an audio-driven soft haptic joystick handle, confirming the technology's capability of relaying haptic information.

Musical Applications. The two fields of haptics and music are naturally connected in a number of ways, from shared perceptual processes and sensory illusions to rich haptic exchanges between musicians and their instruments. A music-to-vibration translation method based on tactile illusions was introduced by Remache-Vinueza et al. which enables vibrotactile stimuli perceived to move and change direction between locations. In the context of gestural control of digital musical instruments (DMI), Järveläinen et al. investigated the potential benefits associated with the provision of vibrotactile feedback via a touch surface on musicians' performance in a pitch bending task. In another DMI study, Rohou–Claquin et al. compared the potential benefits of different methods for rendering vibrotactile feedback on a virtual guitar instrument.

Alongside the 13 papers compiled in this volume, the scientific program of HAID 2022 further included 8 interactive demos (9 proposals were received with one rejected) and 6 work-in-progress posters (2 were re-submissions from the full paper track). Additionally, 4 research workshops/tutorials were co-organised in conjunction with HAID 2022, on haptic-enabled smart assistants, mediated social touch, interactive textiles, and the Bela embedded computing platform. The papers in these proceedings together with the other types of contributions to HAID 2022 reflected promising developments in the field of haptics and audio interaction, but also showed that such research faces several challenges, some of which are common to haptic engineering and human-computer interaction in general, and that much work remains to be done.

August 2022

Charalampos Saitis
Ildar Farkhatdinov
Stefano Papetti

Organization

General Chairs

Charalampos Saitis   Queen Mary University of London, UK
Ildar Farkhatdinov   Queen Mary University of London, UK

Program Chairs

Stefano Papetti   Zürcher Hochschule der Künste, Switzerland
Charalampos Saitis   Queen Mary University of London, UK

Demo Chair

Jacob Harrison   Queen Mary University of London, UK

Diversity and Inclusion Chair

Sophie Skach   Queen Mary University of London, UK

Publicity Chairs

Ildar Farkhatdinov   Queen Mary University of London, UK
Stefano Papetti   Zürcher Hochschule der Künste, Switzerland

Concert Chair

Teresa Pelinski   Queen Mary University of London, UK

Sponsorship Chair

Aaron Smiles   Queen Mary University of London, UK

Website Chair

Francesco Soave   Queen Mary University of London, UK

Advisory Board

Stephen Brewster	University of Glasgow, UK
Nick Bryan-Kinns	Queen Mary University of London, UK
Astrid Kappers	Technische Universiteit Eindhoven, The Netherlands
Marcelo Wanderley	McGill University, Canada
Jonathan Wyner	Berklee College of Music/iZotope, USA

Program Committee

Federico Fontana	Università degli Studi di Udine, Italy
Emma Frid	IRCAM, France
Simon Holland	The Open University, UK
Hanna Järveläinen	Zürcher Hochschule der Künste, Switzerland
Vincent Lévesque	École de technologie supérieure, Canada
Sebastian Merchel	Technische Universität Dresden, Germany
Tychonas Michailidis	Birmingham City University, UK
Lorenzo Picinali	Imperial College London, UK
Thomas Pietrzak	Université de Lille, France
Rebecca Stewart	Imperial College London, UK
Tony Stockman	Queen Mary University of London, UK

Additional Reviewers

Joshua Brown	Razvan Paisa
Doga Cavdir	Simon Perrault
Nathalia Cespedes	Elena Petrovskaya
Bharat Dandu	Myrthe Plaisier
Stefano Delle Monache	Juliette Regimbal
Yuri De Pra	Grégoire Richard
Patrizia Di Campli San Vito	Claire Richards
Balandino Di Donato	Davide Rocchesso
Feng Feng	Robert Rosenkranz
Corey Ford	Pedro Sarmento
Niccolò Granieri	Francesco Soave
David Gueorguiev	Luca Turchet
Michael Hove	Maximilian Weber
Rıza Ilhan	Hong-In Won
Angeliki Mourgela	Chang Xu
Anindya Nag	Gareth W. Young

Sponsoring Institutions

UKRI CDT in AI and Music, Queen Mary University of London, UK
Digital Environment Research Institute, Queen Mary University of London, UK

Contents

Accessibility

TOuch ThE Music: Displaying Live Music into Vibration

Arthur Paté[1]([✉])(iD), Nicolas d'Alessandro[2], Audrey Gréciet[1],
and Clémence Bruggeman[3]

[1] Univ. Lille, CNRS, Centrale Lille, Univ. Polytechnique Hauts-de-France, Junia,
UMR 8520 - IEMN, 59000 Lille, France
arthur.pate@isen.fr
[2] Hovertone, Mons, Belgium
[3] L'Aéronef, Lille, France

Abstract. This paper reports on "TOTEM" (TOuch ThE Music), a
project aiming at finding inclusive solutions to foster the d/Deaf's participation to live music concerts. In particular, the development of a
portable device that transforms live music signals into symbolic vibrations is described. A co-construction, user-centered approach supplied
a list of specifications adapted to the d/Deaf and hearing users' needs.
The specifications were iteratively implemented and discussed over the
course of the project, alternating between developments in the lab and
in situ tests during live music concerts.

Keywords: Vibrotactile display · Deaf · Live music to vibrations

1 Introduction

Listening to live music is an all-times favorite recreational occupation across the
world. Besides, the concert is a major social event, not only because it allows
the access to live music, but also because it is an opportunity to meet people
and engage in other activities than just listening and dancing to the music.
However, the concert as most of us conceive it is still deeply rooted in an audio-
centered paradigm (see e.g. [1]). A major consequence is that the d/Deaf[1] are
implicitly excluded from concerts, whether they themselves decide not to go,
or whether the concert hall is not adapted in terms of equipment or means of
reaching out to the Deaf community. As a result, d/Deaf and hearing people
miss the opportunity to meet at concerts, and the d/Deaf miss an opportunity

---

[1] We use the uppercase "Deaf" to refer to deaf people identifying themselves as belonging to the Deaf culture.

This project was funded by the European Regional Development Funds through the
Interreg FWVL program. The authors thank the users who tested the devices, the
Aéronef's crew and bands, Mur du Son, Gilles Hugo, and students who worked on
earlier versions of the devices.

C. Saitis et al. (Eds.): HAID 2022, LNCS 13417, pp. 3–13, 2022.
https://doi.org/10.1007/978-3-031-15019-7_1

to experience live music, although it is known that music is part of the Deaf culture and practices [4,6]. This paper reports on a collaborative project aiming at finding inclusive solutions to foster the d/Deaf's participation to live music concerts, in both social and technological domains. It focuses however on the latter domain, recounting the development of a device that transforms sound signals into vibrations. Actions in the former domain were implemented too but are not discussed here (see Sect. 1.2).

1.1   Literature on Musical Sound to Vibrotactile Transformation

A comprehensive review of devices and methods that transform musical sounds into vibrotactile signals is beyond the scope of this article and can be found elsewhere [17,22]. The most straightforward and widely used solution is the direct injection of audio signals into speakers mounted onto objects that people touch: vibrating tables and metal rods [3]; pillows, balls, and blankets [13]. The problem of direct injection is that a large part of the audible spectrum is lost, because the human skin is not sensitive to frequencies above 1000 Hz and has a lower frequency resolution than the auditory system (of the order of 10 Hz versus 1 Hz respectively [12]). A solution to overcome these limitations can be to divide the audio signal into several frequency bands, and to map the energy within each band to a specific actuator with a specific signal (often a sine wave within our vibrotactile sensitivity range) [8,9,11]. Another solution requires to "[abstract] the audio signal into a parametric representation" [22, p. 2], i.e. to map audio signal features to features of vibrotactile signals, e.g. audio loudness and roughness mapped to vibrotactile intensity and roughness respectively [10,15]. This abstract mapping is the chosen direction in this article.

A diversity of commercial devices are available for transforming sound into vibrations[2], all advertizing for the enhancement of immersion in music, movies, video games, virtual reality... Some of them, e.g. *Subpac*, have oriented part of their communication on their possible musical use (quite rightfully, see [7]) claiming that their vibrations in the bass frequencies enrich the auditory experience (see Sect. 2 for a discussion): these devices are clearly meant to be used by hearing people as a complement to what they already hear.

The existing literature can also be analyzed in terms of compatibility of the devices or methods to live music conditions. Many studies [8,9,11] use actuators mounted on large furniture (typically an armchair), which is impractical for a use in a concert hall[3]. Besides, the software part itself is often incompatible with the needs of live music, some proposed audio features (e.g. roughness in [10]) are hard to compute in real time. Lastly, note that only a few papers specifically target the d/Deaf's experience, and only a very small part includes them in the

---

[2] E.g. *Bassme*: bassme.com, *Buttkicker*: thebuttkicker.com, *Subpac*: subpac.com, *Basslet*: lofelt.com, *Woojer*: woojer.com .

[3] "[T]he audience etiquette implies that concert-goers stand up and do not necessarily stay at fixed locations during the concert. For this type of settings, haptic wearables may be more suitable than seat-based solutions." [20].

design process [8, 15] (most of the time they can only test a device designed and built without their input).

1.2 Philosophy/approach

Section 1.1 shows a domination of the technological approach (design, develop, assemble a device that converts audio into tactile signals) to a problem that is also social. Unfortunately, even the most advanced technological achievements will never be enough to make the d/Deaf feel entirely comfortable in a concert hall. For this, other, non-technological actions are needed: adapted communication to make the d/Deaf come to an unusual place, work on an artistic programming that is meaningful to the Deaf culture, introduction to the Deaf culture and sign language during the concerts, etc. Partners of this project have different expertises, attempting to cover all these aspects: Junia is a private university with expertise in acoustics; Aéronef is a venue for live contemporary music; Hovertone is a company specialized in the design of interactive exhibitions.

Purely technological approaches to problems often take into account the expert's ideas and knowledge only. In order to avoid this, an approach of inclusion and co-construction is implemented in the project (see Sect. 2): the d/Deaf have directly been involved since the beginning of the project, as well as the d/Deaf and hearing spectators and musicians who joined at each concert.

In order to avoid the pitfall of developing a device that works perfectly in the lab but fails in "real" conditions, this project was conducted from the beginning as much as possible within live conditions, and as an iterative workflow between lab developments and live test sessions (see Sect. 2). This imposes us to use simple but robust algorithms and hardware, but ensures the device does not need radical reshaping when used "in the wild". Our approach is in line with the user-centered design approach, recommending to "[involve] audience members into the design process" [20].

1.3 Goal of This Paper

The main goal of the project is to enhance the d/Deaf's experience of live music, partly through the creation of a device that generates vibrations according to the input live music signal. This paper describes the design of this device, according to the approach explained in Sect. 1.2, and to the guidelines resulting from a critical review of the literature (Sect. 1.1): a) not limit the device to processing low-frequency signals; b) prefer portable devices [20, 23] over immobile vibrating objects; c) include the d/Deaf users from the beginning. Section 2 describes the project's organization, then Sect. 3 presents the specifications for our device, and Sect. 4 presents the technical aspects.

2   Time Line

Phase 1 of the project (Jan. 2019) consisted in 2 d of work between the project partners and the band "Mur du Son"[4], resulting in preliminary devices inspired by the Deaf musicians' behavior with existing vibrotactile devices (*Subpac* already available at Aéronef, exciters of various sizes and powers applied to the skin or to various objects, inflatable balloons, vibrating floors), followed by 1 day of testing by 16 users during the band's concert.

Phase 2 was an alternation between development in the lab and in situ tests during 4 concerts by bands other than "Mur du Son" (validations and changes in the solutions adopted to fulfil the specifications): Jul. 2019, 2 in Nov. 2019, Feb. 2020, each time gathering 7 users in average (total 21 unique users, all fluent in French sign language and part of the Deaf community, without checking for their levels of hearing loss, and including 3 members of "Mur du Son"). User feedback was gathered by writing notes of the interpreter's translation of the users' immediate reactions and remarks. These notes were analyzed during the lab development periods, before updating the device and implementing new features.

Phase 3, a test of the final device during another concert of "Mur du Son", was cancelled due to the Covid-19 crisis. It was replaced by an informal test with a Deaf musician (Dec. 2020) and a concluding webinar[5].

3   Specifications

Observing the behavior of the d/Deaf and hearing users during phase 1, and gathering their feedback, led to a first set of specifications for the device[6]:

- **S1i** Include user-customization options for some features: it might help unfamiliar users to learn and understand the device;
- **S2i** Make the device portable, i.e. the device should not hinder the users' motions, displacements, and social activities during the concert;
- **S3i** Display other aspects of music than rhythm (already conveyed by low-frequency vibrations): users specifically asked for a device that is able to convert aspects like melody or timbre into vibration;
- **S4i** Display other instruments than just drums and bass: focus on middle- or high-frequency instruments that are not usually perceived through vibrations. Users expressed inspiring but challenging wishes, as e.g. "being able to feel a saxophone solo", or "being able to feel different hits on a drum", or the difference between fingers and pick on a guitar".

---

[4] Literally "Sound Barrier", this musical band has only Deaf members (sign language singing, bass guitar, percussions) . Website: https://mur-du-son.fr/.

[5] Available online at https://aeronef.fr/totem/, in French.

[6] First specifications come with a "i" suffix; specifications from iterative user feedback come with a "u" suffix.

Then, additional specifications were made during and after the tests at Aéronef. All of these were initiated by the users, discussed with the researchers, and validated during the next test (or during phase 3)[6]:

- **S5u** (Jul. 2019) Generate vibrotactile signals imitating "textures" (see Sect. 4.2);
- **S6u** (Jul. 2019) Make the vibrotactile stimulation move on the body: define trajectories and map them to an amplitude panning on the actuators;
- **S7u** (Nov. 2019) Focus on separated audio sources and not on the full mix, i.e. process separated channels (associated with visible sound sources on stage) from the mixing desk, and let the user choose the source to display (see **S4i**);
- **S8u** (Nov. 2019) Let the users choose the place of vibratory stimulation (as a function of their age, sex, preferences, etc., and of the proposed stimuli). During tests, users placed the actuators in their hands[7], but also on their chest, abdominal belt, back, thighs, neck, etc., so it was decided not to impose the place for stimulation, and to keep working with actuators simply hanging onto cables that the users can freely handle;
- **S9u** (Feb. 2020) Definition of the presets (see Sect. 4.2), allowing the users to customize their experience;
- **S10u** (Feb. 2020) Provide fully-mobile devices: all parts of the device should be embedded in a single place, that can be taken and held by the user during the whole concert, with no cables attached.

4 Technical Aspects

This section summarizes the technical implementation of the specifications of previous section. As the project ran on limited funding, affordable and widespread hardware was preferred: this actually turns out to be an advantage, since anyone with limited funding and availability of technical staff (small concert venues typically) can afford their own devices. Also, only open source software was used in order to facilitate the diffusion of the device and to foster further developments.

4.1 Hardware

This section describes the final hardware configuration for our device, complying with **S2i** and **S10u** that target a mobile and autonomous device for a better integration in live music venues.

Actuators. Eccentric rotating mass actuators were used at first, for their low mass and low consumption. However, such actuators offer limited possibilities for generating complex signals: limited bandwidth, frequency-dependent output amplitude [5]. Moving-coil actuators were therefore chosen (*Dayton Audio DAEX25CT* actuators, 10W nominal power, low-priced and widely available),

---

[7] Users stated that communication in sign language was not hindered by the manipulation of the actuators.

allowing us to drive the actuators with audio signals, which has conceptual (vibrotactile signals virtually as complex as audio signals) and technological advantages (hardware and software designed for audio purposes can be used).

Audio Processing Chain. A combination of a *Raspberry Pi* computer for analyzing the audio signals and generating the vibrotactile stimuli, a 2-input sound interface *Behringer U-Control UCA222* (48 kHz) and a *XH-M312 TPA3118D2* stereo amplifier (2x45W) was found to meet the requirements of low price, small size, and allow two audio channels from the mixing desk to be processed (**S7u**) and sent to two actuators.

Final Setup. The final device, at a final price of less than 200€, is shown in Figs. 1 (inside) and 2 (carried by a user in a cloth bag). Figure 3 schematically explains how the hardware parts are connected to one another: thanks to batteries and wireless receivers, the cloth bag has no outside cable connection.

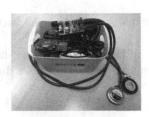

Fig. 1. Hardware part, from top to bottom amplifier, *Raspberry Pi*, sound interface, battery, actuators.

Fig. 2. The final device carried by a user: the cloth bag including the hardware is held on the shoulder, leaving the hands free to manipulate the 2 actuators, possibly using the supplied gloves and wristbands.

4.2   Software

The main aspects of the software[8] in the *Raspberry Pi* are described: first the design of the vibrotactile signals, then the customization through a web interface.
Vibrotactile Signals. The graphical audio programming language Pure Data is chosen for generating the signals: it is well-maintained, open source, and likely to be easier than script languages to users who want to tweak our device.

It was chosen early in phase 1 to abandon the direct injection of sound signals into the actuators: a mixture of instruments with different pitches and timbres may quickly appear as too complex to our tactile system, due to its narrower sensitivity range and higher discrimination thresholds in frequency [12,

---

[8] The code is available at https://github.com/parthurp/TOTEM.

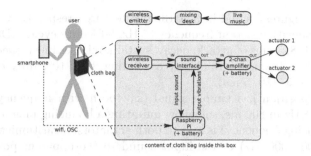

Fig. 3. Schematic view of the hardware part of the device.

21]. Besides, hearing people might relatively quickly learn to recognize pitches, intervals, and timbres from the vibratory signal because they have auditorily experienced these concepts for long, but it is unlikely that people who are deaf since birth categorize the same stimulations as pitches, intervals and timbres, because they don't have a perceptual basis for these concepts. They have "heard" about these aspects of sound and they want stimulations that are different if e.g. the pitch or the timbre changes. It was consequently chosen to generate vibrotactile signals whose characteristics depend on features extracted from the audio.

S5u suggests the design of vibrotactile signals that imitate our perception of "textures", i.e. when touching materials of various roughness. Getting loose inspiration from tribology illustrations and microscope surface imaging , it was thus decided to make the waveform vary as an imitation of a surface that goes from smooth (classical waveform such as a square or an impulse train) to rough (cyclic or random changes in the amplitude, frequency, and duty cycle). It is known that complex waveforms can be discriminated from one another [18]. The texture analogy helped the users familiarize with the signals. As a by-product, the use of different textures prevented the users to get too used to, or even forget the vibrations, an interesting feature for long-term uses of the device.

Once the vibrotactile signals are defined, they remain to be triggered. During the concerts, d/Deaf users focused on melodic or high-frequency instruments (**S4i**), visually recognized various gestures and constantly wondered about how they relate to the sound (e.g. how many notes triggered by one gesture). Vibrotactile signals were thus triggered on each detected event in the sound signal (onset detection made with the **bonk** object in Pure Data).

There is a symbolic relationship (opposed to analogic) between the vibrotactile and audio signals, whose mapping between audio features or musician's gesture and vibrotactile properties is defined by the proposed presets described below. The vibrotactile signals we use share some similarities with tactile icons as in e.g. [19], but their characteristics are piloted by the input signal.

- Preset 1 (displayed to the user as "rugosité"—roughness): a signal is sent to both actuators, with one of two available textures, depending on the comparison of the audio spectral centroid (hereafter SC, [14]) with a threshold value of 1500 Hz. Figures 5 a and b show the two textures, respectively for a low SC (square wave with constant frequency 35 Hz, 50% duty cycle, ADSR envelope with 50, 2, 148, 50 ms of attack, decay, sustain, release time respectively), and for a high SC (frequency randomly oscillating 8 Hz, 10% duty cycle, ADSR with times 5, 5, 150, 5 ms).

- Preset 2 ("position"): a simple signal (sawtooth with frequency decreasing from 30 to 8 Hz in 800 ms, somehow imitating a bouncing pingpong ball, but with decreasing frequency) is sent to both actuators, logarithmically mapping the SC (400–8000 Hz) of the input sound to the apparent position of the vibration source between actuators using the VBAP technique [16] (left-right panning).
- Preset 3 ("caresse"—cuddle): a square wave with frequency proportional (scale factor 200) to the spectral flatness [14] of the input signal is mixed with an order-3, 500 Hz low-pass white noise: the SC of the input signal controls the balance (linear mapping 0 Hz—square wave only to 5000 Hz—noise only).
- Preset 4 ("balayage"—sweeping): Using VBAP, a signal with a fixed texture (square wave with frequency randomly picked in the range 10–30 Hz) moves from actuator 1 to actuator 2 for each even-numbered detected audio onset, and from 2 to 1 for odd-numbered onsets. Alternating the direction of vibro-tactile motion mimicks the strumming gesture of guitar players.
- Preset 5 ("multiple"): onsets from one input channel trigger vibrotactile signals into one actuator (square wave of 150 Hz, ADSR with times 20, 0, 48, and 2 ms), and similarly for the other input channel into the other actuator (square wave of 200 Hz, ADSR with times 5, 5, 50, and 10 ms). This feature can help discriminating sound sources by making their associated vibrations appear at different places.

Remote Control. With their smartphones, the users can connect to the device over a WIFI connection. A webpage hosted by each *Raspberry Pi* allows the user to choose the input sound to be processed (2 inputs available), select one of the 5 presets described above (only one active at a time), control the "sensitivity" of the algorithm for the onset detection and the output volume of the vibrations.

5   Concluding Discussion and Future Work

The project results in six devices available at Aéronef on concert evenings. Following the Covid-19 pandemic, the live music activities are just being resumed at the time of writing, and therefore no formal final user test could be performed. This section lists general observations made during the project.

The freedom in the manipulation of actuators and the customization through the web interface allow different users with different sensitivities to adapt the device to their own needs. It also permits users to share their experiences, by passing the actuators to each other, or touching the same actuator at the same time (see Fig. 4). Throughout the project, it was striking to observe that users

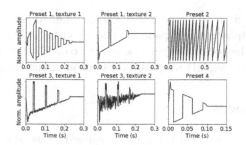

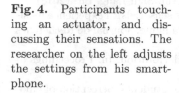

Fig. 4. Participants touching an actuator, and discussing their sensations. The researcher on the left adjusts the settings from his smartphone.

Fig. 5. Example waveforms of vibrotactile signals corresponding to presets 1 (a, b), 2 (c), 3 (d, e), 4 (f).

need to share their sensations. On the contrary to auditory experience, the vibrotactile experience proposed here is a very new experience, which seems to need a collective approach in order to become familiar and cognitively accepted.

The Deaf musicians also had the idea of using the vibrotactile feedback as a complement to onstage monitors. In order to create enough vibrations, d/Deaf musicians must play at very loud sound levels, making it very difficult for the sound technicians to reach a satisfactory sound balance. Using actuators on specific body parts that each display specific instruments (**S7u**) improved the comfort of performing d/Deaf musicians in terms of sound balance. Such an application of vibrotactile feedback may be useful to hearing musicians too, as the fine setting of onstage monitoring is known to be challenging.

Finally, users who tested the device at each development step acknowledged the evolution towards "richer" and "finer" vibrations allowing the perception of "vibratory details that were not present at the beginning" (selected wordings from some participants: formal tests may be conducted to assess how these statements are representative of the whole pool of users, and what they precisely mean). This partly validates the choices to focus on higher frequency ranges, free actuator location, and original principles for rendering vibrotactile signals: the devices's behavior can be learnt by users in a reasonable amount of time (a couple of hours in our case). These choices also allow our device to be used as a complement to other devices (e.g. with the *Subpac* in Fig. 4) focused on different frequency ranges, sound sources, and body locations. Challenges for future work remain, e.g. to fulfill the d/Deaf users' wish for a vibrotactile display of the melody, or to use the final mix as audio input (no separate instruments).

There also is a need to go further into the co-construction of the devices : if the d/Deaf use the device for accessing music as its sonic aspect, the device may also be used to make hearing people discover the diversity of Deaf music! Briceno advocates for the creation of a novel art form based on the sense of touch, free from audio-centered conceptions of music, in order to overcome the conception of music as a "sensory reductionism", i.e. music either reduced to its audible dimension by hearing people, or to its visual dimension by Deaf people [2]. The work in the present paper is a modest contribution to this idea, if conceiving the vibrotactile signals we propose as autonomous tactile objects.

References

1. Best, K.: Musical belonging in a hearing-centric society: adapting and contesting dominant cultural norms through deaf hip hop. J. Am. Sign Lang. Lit. (2018)
2. Briceno, A.: La musique au-delà des réductionnismes sensoriels?: l'expérience musicale des sourds comme fondement d'un nouveau paradigme. Journal de Recherches en Éducation musicale **12**(2), 36–46 (2021)
3. Criton, P.: Listening otherwise: Playing with sound vibration. In: Proceedings of ICMC/SMC, pp. 1805–1808. Athens, Greece (2014)
4. Darrow, A.A.: The role of music in deaf culture: deaf students' perception of emotion in music. J. Music Ther. **43**(1), 2–15 (2006)
5. Giordano, M., et al.: Design and implementation of a whole-body haptic suit for "ilinx", a multisensory art installation. In: Proceedings of SMC, pp. 169–175 (2015)
6. Holmes, J.A.: Expert listening beyond the limits of hearing. J. Am. Musicological Soc. **70**(1), 171–220 (2017)
7. Hove, M.J., Martinez, S.A., Stupacher, J.: Feel the bass: music presented to tactile and auditory modalities increases aesthetic appreciation and body movement. J. Exp. Psychol. Gen. **149**(6), 1137–1147 (2020)
8. Jack, R., McPherson, A., Stockman, T.: Designing tactile musical devices with and for deaf users: a case study. In: Proceedings of the International Conference on the Multimodal Experience of Music (ICMEM) (2015)
9. Karam, M., Russo, F.A., Fels, D.I.: Designing the model human cochlea: an ambient crossmodal audio-tactile display. IEEE Trans. Haptics **2**(3), 160–169 (2009)
10. Lee, J., Choi, S.: Real-time perception-level translation from audio signals to vibrotactile effects. In: Proceedings of CHI, pp. 2567–2576. Paris, France (2013)
11. Merchel, S., Altinsoy, M.E.: Auditory-tactile music perception. In: Proceedings of the International Congress on Acoustics. Montreal, QC, Canada (2013)
12. Merchel, S., Altinsoy, M.E.: Psychophysical comparison of the auditory and tactile perception: a survey. J. Multimodal User Interfaces **14**(3), 271–283 (2020). https://doi.org/10.1007/s12193-020-00333-z
13. Patiño-Lakatos, G., et al.: Music, vibrotactile mediation and bodily sensations in anorexia nervosa. Hum. Technol. **16**(3), 372–405 (2020)
14. Peeters, G.: A large set of audio features for sound description. Technical Report, IRCAM, Paris, France (2004)
15. Petry, B., Illandara, T., Forero, J.P., Nanayakkara, S.: Ad-hoc access to musical sound for deaf individuals. In: Proceedings of ASSETS 2016, Reno, NV, USA (2016)
16. Pulkki, V.: Virtual sound source positioning using vector base amplitude panning. J. Audio Eng. Soc. **45**(6), 456–466 (1997)
17. Remache-Vinueza, B., Trujillo-León, A., Zapata, M., Sarmiento-Ortiz, F., Fernando, V.V.: Audio-tactile rendering: a review on technology and methods to convey musical information through the sense of touch. Sensors **21**(16), 6575 (2021)
18. Russo, F.A., Ammirante, P., Fels, D.I.: Vibrotactile discrimination of musical timbre. J. Exp. Psych. Hum. Percept. Perform. **32**(4), 822–826 (2012)

19. Shim, S.-W., Tan, H.Z.: palmScape: calm and pleasant vibrotactile signals. In: Marcus, A., Rosenzweig, E. (eds.) HCII 2020. LNCS, vol. 12200, pp. 532–548. Springer, Cham (2020). https://doi.org/10.1007/978-3-030-49713-2_37
20. Turchet, L., West, T., Wanderley, M.M.: Touching the audience: musical haptic wearables for augmented and participatory live music performances. Pers. Ubiquit. Comput. 25(4), 749–769 (2020). https://doi.org/10.1007/s00779-020-01395-2
21. Verrillo, R.T.: Vibration sensation in humans. Music Percept. Interdisc. J. 9(3), 282–302 (1992)
22. Weber, M., Saitis, C.: Towards a framework for ubiquitous audio-tactile design. In: International Workshop on Haptic and Audio Interaction Design. Montreal, Canada (2020)
23. West, T.J., Bachmayer, A., Bhagwati, S., Berzowska, J., Wanderley, M.M.: The design of the body:suit:score, a full-body vibrotactile musical score. In: Yamamoto, S., Mori, H. (eds.) HCII 2019. LNCS, vol. 11570, pp. 70–89. Springer, Cham (2019). https://doi.org/10.1007/978-3-030-22649-7_7

Tickle Tuner - Haptic Smartphone Cover for Cochlear Implant Users' Musical Training

Francesco Ganis[1,2](✉) (iD), Marianna Vatti[3], and Stefania Serafin[1,2](iD)

[1] Aalborg University, A. C. Mayers Vænge 15, 2450 København, Denmark
francesco.ganis@gmail.com, sts@create.aau.dk
[2] Multisensory Experience Lab, A. C. Mayers Vænge 15, 2450 København, Denmark
[3] Oticon Medical, Kongebakken 9, 2765 Smørum, Denmark
mvat@oticonmedical.com

Abstract. Cochlear implants (CIs) allow individuals that can no longer benefit from hearing aids to understand speech with remarkable efficiency. On the other hand, they perform poorly in music perception. Previous research suggest that music experience can be enhanced with the use of other senses such as touch. We present Tickle Tuner, a haptic feedback device suitable for musical training of CI users. The prototype is composed of two high-quality haptic actuators and an external Digital to Analogue Converter (DAC) hosted in a 3D printed enclosure coupled with a smartphone. We describe the design and implementation of the prototype and the analysis of its characteristics. We introduce a test bench for the design of different mappings between sound and vibrations which we assessed with a Melodic Contour Identification (MCI) task. Results from a group of fifteen normal hearing participants using CIs simulation showed significantly higher performance (increase of 26% more correct answers) with haptic feedback than without.

Keywords: Haptic feedback · Cochlear implants · Musical training

1 Introduction

Cochlear implants (CIs) are neuroprosthesis that allow people with severe or profound hearing loss to restore their sound perception. They are especially successful in reestablishing speech comprehension [6]. Music is a highly complex phenomenon and during the electrical stimulation of the auditory pathway, there are many factors that can influence CI users' access and enjoyment [5,18,19]. These limitations are translated into reduced pitch range and lack of low frequencies, incapability of distinguish consonance and dissonance [15]. However, there is emerging evidence that music training may improve music perception

---

In collaboration with Oticon Medical.

skills and enjoyment [15]. One of the novel techniques to improve musical listening performance is the use of haptic feedback [8]. While vibrotactile feedback for speech understanding has a long history, starting with the pioneering work of Cowan et al. [3], the same cannot be said for musical appreciation connected to hearing impairment. Studies have shown that haptics improve melody recognition [20], instrument identification [23] and emotional communication [17]. Additionally, haptics have been shown to improve speech-in-noise performance and sound localization [9,10]. One of the most crucial parts of this project is how the haptics are coupled with sound. The vibrotactile sensitivity is affected by several parameters such as location of the stimuli, dimension of the contact area and type of signal [16,26]. In addition, other perceptive and physiological characteristics such as temporal masking and energy integration make even more difficult to disentangle the correlation between haptics and sound [21]. Thus, we hope that different mappings and user tests will help to clarify the situation, finding correspondence between audio and haptic cues. Haptic feedback is widely used in video game consoles and smartphones to enhance the visual content and Singhal and Schneider [24] propose a vibrotactile embellishment to improve the overall player's experience. In Weber and Saitis' work [27] a conceptual framework and different methods are proposed to translate audio to vibrotactile feedback. Other researchers found inspiration directly from the natural haptic feedback conveyed through musical instruments [2] or propose to use Digital Signal Processing (DSP) techniques to extrapolate audio features and re-map them to haptic features [1]. Finally, Dementyev et al. [4] propose a vibrotactile haptic platform with some practical applications.

In this paper we propose the Tickle Tuner, a vibrotactile feedback device that provides haptic information during musical training that can be performed using *ad hoc* mobile games. These applications are developed for improving CIs skills to better recognize musical features and thus increase music appreciation. The name of our prototype derives from the Tickle Talker, the first device that uses haptic feedback to aid speech understanding [3]. The prototype presented was developed after considering the limitations of different projects such as wristbands, vests [13,28] or haptic actuators embedded in furniture [25] (chairs and sofas). The wearable solutions (e.g. wristbands and vests), require the user to wear an additional device and can elicit potentially uncomfortable experiences whereas haptic chairs and sofas bound the user to a specific location. Hence we focused on designing a prototype for mobile phones since they are part of most of our daily activities, from work to entertainment. We aimed for an external device, as the actuators available in smartphones are limited in bandwidth and linearity, and the overall performance varies a lot among models [27].

2   Prototype Design and Implementation

The smartphone cover is mainly composed by two parts: shell and handles. The shell features an adjustable rail system and a frame that holds in position the smartphone, connects the two handles and hosts part of the cables. The handles are the main contact area with the user's hands and should be shaped in order to have a stable and comfortable grip. We choose the 3D printing technology to obtain a durable and comfortable object since it is possible to use plastic materials and a good reproduction quality can be easily achieved. For our prototype we used polylactic acid (PLA), a common and affordable thermoplastic polyester used for 3D prints. The whole process involved four different software and an iterative approach between a print and the next design. The Tickle Tuner is tailored-made for the Android phone Poco X3 NFC but it can be easily adapted to other smartphones or even tablets.

The skeleton has a fairly simple form with only some cavities to accommodate cables and rubber bands. Its shape can be easily represented by sum and subtraction of primitives. For this reason, we choose OpenSCAD[1] since it allows the user to create 3D models with this intuitive technique. In future developments and adaptations to different devices (e.g. different smartphones), we will be able to rapidly change dimensions and proportions of our prototype between each iteration only using the user defined variables in the software. The skeleton is divided in two parts, each of them corresponding to one handle. To connect both sides, we used a single rail system where two cuboids slide inside each other pulled by the force exerted by a rubber band. Two T shaped hooks are placed on the smallest rail and a track is engraved on the biggest one to hold in place the rails and preventing them from moving on y and z axes. On the right side, we equipped the skeleton with a lid and some space underneath to place an external DAC. The lid can be easily secured or removed with two screws.

The handles have great importance in the design process since we aimed to have a steady and comfortable grip as possible. We used clay to mold a prototype of a handle, focusing on its ergonomic shape and on the fingers' grooves. Once we obtained a satisfying result, we used photogrammetry to reconstruct a digital version of the model. Finally, we loaded the pictures in Meshroom[2] to retrieve the digital model. The reconstruction was ported into a Blender[3] to remove some irregularities and artifacts created during the photogrammetry process. Since the handles are in direct contact with the user's skin, we inserted a small box that perfectly contains the Haptuators. We filled the gaps with PLA connecting three sides of each haptic actuator box to the handle in order to conduct the highest amount of vibrations as possible.

Once we obtained the digital version of the skeleton and the handles, we ported them into Blender project to produce a model suitable for the 3D print. Using a Ultimaker 3 printer[4] with the fastest settings as possible, we were able to print the whole prototype in approximately 12.30 h using 100 g of PLA.

---

[1] https://openscad.org, last access July 18, 2022.
[2] https://alicevision.org/#meshroom, last access July 18, 2022.
[3] https://www.blender.org/, last access July 18, 2022.
[4] https://ultimaker.com/3d-printers/ultimaker-3, last access July 18, 2022.

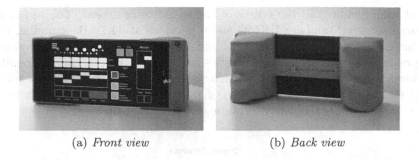

(a) *Front view*   (b) *Back view*

Fig. 1. The tickle tuner prototype.

2.1   Circuitry

The Tickle Tuner features two HapCoil-One (Haptuator Mark II-D) actuators produced by Actronika[5] that can reproduce frequencies from 10 10000 Hz. They are both connected to a 3W stereo class-D amplifier PAM8403 chip on a DFR0119 board. This amplifier perfectly fits our needs since features low THD+N, low power consumption and two output channels. The smartphone feeds the Haptuators through a digital to analog converter chip (DAC) that receives the audio stream through a USB-C plug. We slightly modified the DAC soldering two cables from the pin-out of the USB-C connector to retrieve DC (+5V) and ground (GND) for powering the amplifier. In this way, with a single plug the Tickle Tuner is able to retrieve the audio signal and the power recalling the *plug and play* concept.

2.2   Analysis

In order to understand the acoustical characteristics of the Tickle Tuner, we measured its frequency response. Following the guidelines of Farina at al. [7], we wrote a MATLAB script that generates a exponentially-swept sine signal following the equation:

$$x(t) = \sin\left(\frac{\omega \cdot T}{\ln\left(\frac{\omega_2}{\omega_1}\right)} \cdot \left(e^{\frac{t}{T} \cdot \ln\left(\frac{\omega_2}{\omega_1}\right) - 1} \right) \right) \tag{1}$$

The sine sweeps are repeated in order to perform an average of all the sweeps reducing the noise effect of the recordings and thus improving the Signal-To-Noise ration (S/N) [7]. We performed the measurements in an anechoic room located at Aalborg University Copenhagen to prevent any noise from altering the results. We placed an analog accelerometer (Sparkfun ADXL335) on seven different areas of the device and recorded the vibrations from one single output axe of the accelerometer. The areas taken into account are: top, bottom and

---

[5] https://www.actronika.com/, last access July 18, 2022.

side of each handle and the center of the smartphone screen. The signal was captured using a Stainberg UR44C audio interface at 44.1 kHz sampling rate. The impulse responses retrieved from the different locations are fairly similar and present some common characteristics such as a peak in the low range 70 Hz and lower energy in the highest section of the spectra. The average of all the repetitions in all the seven locations is reported in Fig. 2 and from now on we will refer to it as the frequency response of the Tickle Tuner.

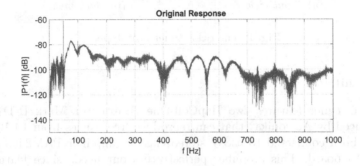

Fig. 2. Frequency response of the Tickle Tuner.

2.3   Filter Design

Feeding the Tickle Tuner with unfiltered audio from the smartphone creates a satisfactory haptic feedback that is possibly enhanced by a video source. The device provides robust low frequency vibrations and we expect that it will contribute towards improving the perception of the lowest portion of the sound spectra in CIs users. In order to mitigate the unwanted resonances of our device, we designed 7 biquad filters of the second order. In addition, we developed a second filter that compensates the fingertips' sensibility attenuating the mid-low range of the spectra with a center frequency 250 Hz [16].

3   Methods

In the following section of the paper we will discuss the test of MCI mapping.

3.1   Participants

Fifteen normal hearing participants were selected through convenient sampling of which 13 males and 2 females (age M = 28.3, STD = 4.7). The participants self reported an average of 13.5 years of musical experience (STD = 9.7).

3.2 Stimuli and Mappings

To design the experiment, we initially investigated different mappings developing a test bench in Pure Data[6] coupled with a Graphical User Interface (GUI) using the platform MobMuPlat[7] to have a comfortable access to the parameters from the touchscreen. The software currently features several functionalities such as waves generators (sine, square, triangle, saw-tooth), subtractive synthesizer, ADSR control and sequencer, audio player, pitch tracking algorithm (with 4 controllable partials), filters for frequency response compensation and fingertips sensitivity compensation. Every generator has its own knob for controlling the fundamental frequency. The filter for the subtractive synthesis features also a knob for the quality (Q) factor. All the audio sources have separate volume control and independent routing to the audio and the haptics' channels. The filters are the same implemented in MATLAB (2.3) and are applied only to the haptics channel to leave the audio signal untouched. One specific mapping born after some iterations and with the test bench is the amplitude modulation of the first partial estimated through the *sigmund* $\sim$ object. This approach has been inspired by Park and Choi [14] work where they investigate the perceptual relations between amplitude modulated signals conveyed through haptics. The algorithm implemented applies amplitude modulation to the fundamental frequency f_0 with the modulating frequency f_m directly dependent from the f_0. The minimum and maximum frequencies can be set accordingly to the user's needs and the final f_m is thus scaled proportionally in a range between 0 20 Hz. The AM method used is called *Double-sideband suppressed carrier* (DBSC) since the modulated signal presents two sidebands with half the energy of the carrier.

To test this mapping, We chose four different sound sources to cover different ranges of the spectrum and timbre combinations. The clarinet and viola sound stimuli were generated using the Audio Modeling SWAM plug-in suite[8] that uses a combination of physical models and recorded samples to obtain an extremely convincing simulation of real instruments. The piano was recorded using the Addictive Keys Grand Piano plug-in[9] that uses recorded samples and a large variety of microphones. The last sound source is a simple sine wave generated from a MATLAB script. Each MIDI melodic contour was played through the above mentioned plug-ins using a sample rate of 44.1 kHz and 16 bit of depth. Moreover, we used the Cochlear Implant Simulator AngelSim[TM][10] with a 8-channel noise vocoded speech simulation to modify the audio stimuli and simulate how a cochlear implant might sound. We used three different mappings: the Amplitude Modulation, full audio through the haptic actuators and no haptics.

---

[6] https://puredata.info/, last access July 18, 2022.

[7] https://danieliglesia.com/mobmuplat/, last access July 18, 2022.

[8] https://audiomodeling.com/swam-engine/, last access July 18, 2022.

[9] https://www.xlnaudio.com/products/addictive_keys, last access July 18, 2022.

[10] http://www.tigerspeech.com/angelsim/angelsim_about, last access July 18, 2022.

3.3 MCI Test Variant

This test was developed to investigate the effect of the amplitude modulation on the perceived pitch using different sound sources. We developed a *Melodic Contour Identification* (MCI) task inspired by Galvin et al. [11,12] and Omran et al. [22]. The test was designed with a similar interface to the testbench using PureData and MobMuPlat. In this way, the participants interacted directly on the Tickle Tuner's for the whole duration of the test. For this setup, we selected six different melodic contours. The played notes ranged from C3 (130.81 Hz) to G3# (207.65 Hz). The different combinations were written into MIDI files using Reaper[11] to later feed different audio plug-ins. Each note lasted one quarter at 120 beats per minute (0.5 s) and the contours were generated with one or two semitones of distance between each note. Thus, the test used twelve different melodic contours (6 contour types × 2 distances between each note).

3.4 Procedures

The test was conducted in an anechoic room of the Aalborg University Campus in Copenhagen. Before the beginning of the test, each participant experienced a mock session to get acquainted with the interface and the mechanics of the test. The training page, with the same aspect of the test page, showed to the participants the different combination of contours. Once the next contour was generated, it was possible to listen to the correspondent melody played by the piano (without CI simulation) as well as feel the AM mapping on the haptic actuators. For every contour, the GUI highlighted the correct answer with a green label. The training session lasted approximately 2 min and no information regarding how the mappings work or which sound sources has been used were shared with the participants before the end of the test.

4 Results and Discussion

The collected data present no correlation between the musical experience and the scores obtained during the MCI task with CI simulation (correlation coefficient = 0.37). This might be explained because the contours are extremely difficult to recognize when there is a small distance between each note (semitone and tone) and a CI simulation is used [12]. Figure 3a shows the pooled results for all the instruments and the two possible distances between the notes (1 or 2 semitones) combined. AM mapping has a mean score of 65% correct answers while CI (only audio) is 45% and no haptic 38.33%. Running an one-way ANOVA test and t-tests on pairs of data sets, it is noticeable a significant difference between all the data, with a p-value $\ll 0.05$. This initial analysis shows a good performance of the Amplitude Modulation mapping, remembering that the participants did not receive any information about how the mappings work. In Fig. 3b and 3c scores for all the instruments are depicted with one and two semitones respectively.

---

[11] https://www.reaper.fm/, last access July 18, 2022.

Comparing the two graphs, it is possible to notice that the two semitones are easier to recognize (as expected), and in the two semitones answers there is no significant difference between the full audio and the no haptic feedback mappings. Moreover, the users scored an average of approximately 10% better results with two semitones than with one semitone on the AM mapping. Running a t-test analysis on each mapping comparing the percentage of correct answer for one against two semitones, significant difference (p-value < 0.05) has been found in both AM and NoH mappings while for CI the semitone change does not have any effect.

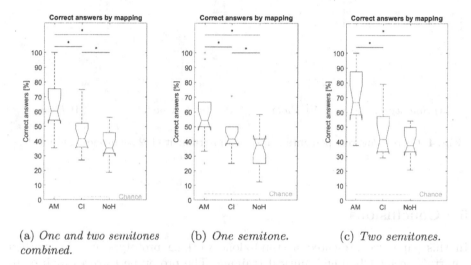

(a) *One and two semitones combined.*   (b) *One semitone.*   (c) *Two semitones.*

Fig. 3. Percentage of correct answers, where AM is the amplitude modulation mapping, CI is the full audio through haptics and NoH is no haptic feedback.

In Fig. 4 we present the answers filtered by instrument to show how the mappings affected the percentage of correct answer in each condition. The sine wave scored close to 80% for each mapping. This can be explained thanks to the fact that the CIs simulation can adequately reproduce a simple sine wave and most probably the users used mainly the sound stimuli to recognize the correct contour. Removing the sine wave from the data set, a bigger interaction between instrument and mappings is noticeable since AM mappings achieved a mean of 59.07% and audio only mapping 32.78% (gap of 26.29%). Looking at the other instruments, a common trait is the non-significant difference between the full audio (CI) and the no haptics mappings that scored both a low median value of correct answers. The viola (Fig. 4b) has the most evident gap between the AM and the other two mappings. Moreover, full audio and no haptics mapping were very difficult to recognize, most probably due to the specific spectral characteristics of the instrument (the fundamental frequency is not very pronounced).

The test demonstrated the validity of the Amplitude Modulation mapping to better convey pitch information without any user training compared to no haptic feedback. On the other hand, some limitations should be also highlighted. In fact, the pool of subjects is modest and the CIs simulation is a mere hardware simulation that cannot take into account the very personal hearing panorama that each person with CIs experiences.

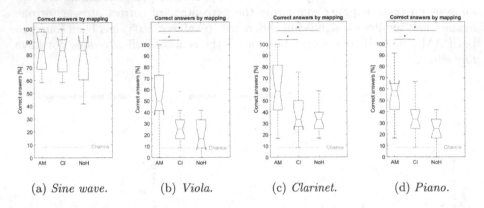

(a) *Sine wave.*   (b) *Viola.*   (c) *Clarinet.*   (d) *Piano.*

Fig. 4. Correct answers percentage for each instrument (1–2 semitones combined).

5   Conclusions

In this paper we presented a stand-alone working prototype coupled with a smartphone for CIs users' musical training. The prototype features high quality haptic feedback with an ergonomic interaction. We recorded its frequency response and created a multi-band equalizer to compensate internal resonances and spectral irregularities. Furthermore, we designed a test bench to facilitate the process of audio-haptic mappings creation and designed an audio-haptic mapping suitable for melodic contour identification tasks. We plan to upgrade the prototype with both hardware and software improvements and to conduct further tests to assess its effectiveness in musical training for CI.

References

1. Birnbaum, D.M., Wanderley, M.M.: A systematic approach to musical vibrotactile feedback, p. 8 (2011)
2. Chafe, C.: Tactile audio feedback. In: Proceedings of the International Computer Music Conference, pp. 76–76. International computer music accociation (1993)
3. Cowan, R.S., Sarant, J.Z., Galvin, K.L., Alcantara, J.I., Blamey, P.J., Clark, G.M.: The tickle talker: a speech perception aid for profoundly hearing impaired children. Sci. Publ. **5**(300), 1989–1990 (1990)
4. Dementyev, A., Getreuer, P., Kanevsky, D., Slaney, M., Lyon, R.: VHP: vibrotactile haptics platform for on-body applications, p. 15 (2021)

5. Drennan, W.R., et al.: Clinical evaluation of music perception, appraisal and experience in cochlear implant users. Int. J. Audiol. **54**(2), 114–123 (2015). https://doi.org/10.3109/14992027.2014.948219
6. Zeng, F.G., Rebscher, S., Harrison, W., Sun, X., Feng, H.,: Cochlear implants: system design, integration, and evaluation. IEEE Rev. Biomed. Eng. **1**, 115–142 (2008). https://doi.org/10.1109/RBME.2008.2008250
7. Farina, A.: Simultaneous measurement of impulse response and distortion with a swept-sine technique, p. 24 (2000)
8. Fletcher, M.D.: Can haptic stimulation enhance music perception in hearing-impaired listeners? Front. Neurosci. **15**, 723877 (2021). https://doi.org/10.3389/fnins.2021.723877
9. Fletcher, M.D., Cunningham, R.O., Mills, S.R.: Electro-haptic enhancement of spatial hearing in cochlear implant users. Sci. Rep. **10**(1), 1621 (2020). https://doi.org/10.1038/s41598-020-58503-8
10. Fletcher, M.D., Hadeedi, A., Goehring, T., Mills, S.R.: Electro-haptic enhancement of speech-in-noise performance in cochlear implant users. Sci. Rep. **9**(1), 11428 (2019). https://doi.org/10.1038/s41598-019-47718-z
11. Galvin, J.J., Fu, Q.J., Nogaki, G.: Melodic contour identification by cochlear implant listeners. Ear Hear. **28**(3), 302–319 (2007). https://doi.org/10.1097/01.aud.0000261689.35445.20
12. Galvin, J.J., Fu, Q.J., Shannon, R.V.: Melodic contour identification and music perception by cochlear implant users. Ann. N. Y. Acad. Sci. **1169**(1), 518–533 (2009). https://doi.org/10.1111/j.1749-6632.2009.04551.x
13. Garcia-Valle, G., Ferre, M., Brenosa, J., Vargas, D.: Evaluation of presence in virtual environments: haptic vest and user's haptic skills. IEEE Access **6**, 7224–7233 (2018). https://doi.org/10.1109/ACCESS.2017.2782254
14. Park, G., Choi, S.: Perceptual space of amplitude-modulated vibrotactile stimuli. In: 2011 IEEE World Haptics Conference, pp. 59–64. IEEE, Istanbul, June 2011. https://doi.org/10.1109/WHC.2011.5945462
15. Jiam, N.T., Caldwell, M.T., Limb, C.J.: What does music sound like for a cochlear implant user? Otol. Neurotology **38**(8), e240–e247 (2017). https://doi.org/10.1097/MAO.0000000000001448
16. Jones, L.A., Sarter, N.B.: Tactile displays: guidance for their design and application. Hum. Fact. J. Hum. Fact. Ergon. Soc. **50**(1), 90–111 (2008). https://doi.org/10.1518/001872008X250638
17. Karam, M., Russo, F., Fels, D.: Designing the model human cochlea: an ambient crossmodal audio-tactile display. IEEE Trans. Haptics **2**(3), 160–169 (2009). https://doi.org/10.1109/TOH.2009.32
18. Limb, C.J., Roy, A.T.: Technological, biological, and acoustical constraints to music perception in cochlear implant users. Hear. Res. **308**, 13–26 (2014). https://doi.org/10.1016/j.heares.2013.04.009
19. Looi, V., Mcdermott, H., McKay, C.M., Hickson, L.: The effect of cochlear implantation on music perception by adults with usable pre-operative acoustic hearing. Int. J. Audiol. **47**, 257–268 (2008)
20. Luo, X., Hayes, L.: Vibrotactile stimulation based on the fundamental frequency can improve melodic contour identification of normal-hearing listeners with a 4-channel cochlear implant simulation. Front. Neurosci. **13**, 1145 (2019). https://doi.org/10.3389/fnins.2019.01145
21. Merchel, S., Altinsoy, M.E.: Psychophysical comparison of the auditory and tactile perception: a survey. J. Multi. User Interfaces **14**(3), 271–283 (2020). https://doi.org/10.1007/s12193-020-00333-z

22. Omran, S.A., Lai, W., Dillier, N.: Pitch ranking, melody contour and instrument recognition tests using two semitone frequency maps for nucleus cochlear implants. EURASIP J. Audio Speech Music Process. **2010**(1), 1–16 (2010). https://doi.org/10.1155/2010/948565
23. Russo, F.A., Ammirante, P., Fels, D.I.: Vibrotactile discrimination of musical timbre. J. Exp. Psychol. Hum. Percept. Perform. **38**(4), 822–826 (2012). https://doi.org/10.1037/a0029046
24. Singhal, T., Schneider, O.: Juicy haptic design: vibrotactile embellishments can improve player experience in games, p. 11 (2021)
25. Tan, H.Z., Gray, R., Young, J.J., Traylor, R.: A haptic back display for attentional and directional cueing, p. 20 (2003)
26. Verrillo, R.T.: Vibration sensation in humans. Music Percept. **9**(3), 281–302 (1992). https://doi.org/10.2307/40285553
27. Weber, M., Saitis, C.: Towards a framework for ubiquitous audio-tactile design, p. 9 (2020)
28. Wu, J., Zhang, J., Yan, J., Liu, W., Song, G.: Design of a vibrotactile vest for contour perception. Int. J. Adv. Rob. Syst. **9**(5), 166 (2012). https://doi.org/10.5772/52373

Phonemic-based Tactile Supplement to Lipreading: Initial Findings on Consonant Identification

Charlotte M. Reed[1]([✉])[iD], Dimitri Kanevsky[2][iD], Joseph G. Desloge[3][iD],
Juan S. Martinez[4][iD], and Hong Z. Tan[4][iD]

[1] Research Lab of Electronics, Massachusetts Institute of Technology,
Cambridge, MA 02139, USA
cmreed@mit.edu
[2] Google Research, Mountain View, CA 94043, USA
dkanevsky@google.com
[3] San Francisco, CA, USA
[4] Haptic Interface Research Lab, Purdue University,
West Lafayette, IN 47907, USA
{mart1304,hongtan}@purdue.edu

Abstract. We present the initial results of a 7-channel tactile aid worn
on the forearm, which was designed as a supplement to lipreading. Consonant confusion patterns through lipreading alone were first assessed
in one non-native English speaker with profound deafness. A phonemic-
based tactile coding scheme was then developed to disambiguate sets of
two or more speech sounds that appear similar on the lips (i.e., visemes).
After a period of training with the tactile aid in combination with lipreading, scores for identification of a set of 22 consonants were substantially
higher for the aided lipreading condition (74%-correct) than through
lipreading alone (44%-correct). This performance compares favorably to
that reported in the literature for spectral-based tactile aids. These initial results demonstrate the potential of a phonemic-based approach to
a tactile supplement of lipreading.

Keywords: Tactile aid · Phoneme-based · Lipreading · Supplement ·
Deafness

1 Introduction

Based on statistics provided by the World Health Organization, there are roughly
12 to 25 million persons worldwide with profound deafness. Roughly 1 million
Americans are estimated to be "functionally deaf," that is, unable to hear normal
conversation even with a hearing aid [8]. Severe-to-profound hearing impairment

Research supported by an award to MIT from Google LLC for work by C.M. Reed on
"Wearable Tactile Displays." It is also partially supported by NSF Grants IIS 1954886
(to MIT) and 1954842 (to Purdue).

C. Saitis et al. (Eds.): HAID 2022, LNCS 13417, pp. 25–34, 2022.
https://doi.org/10.1007/978-3-031-15019-7_3

has serious ramifications throughout the life cycle, with negative effects observed in terms of level of income, activity, education, and employment [15]. While some profoundly deaf individuals use sign language for communication, other deaf children and adults rely mainly on oral methods of communication. For those individuals who do not have sufficient residual hearing to derive benefit from traditional hearing aids, other prosthetic devices are available to provide spoken language to children and adults with profound deafness, including cochlear implants and tactual aids.

Although performance with current wearable tactual aids is often inferior to that achieved with cochlear implants [10], not all deaf persons who rely on spoken language are able to be implanted or to achieve benefits from implantation. Speech-to-text applications, now readily available for use on smartphones, also provide Deaf and Hard-of-Hearing persons access to spoken language. However, a need still exists for face-to-face communication without the use of captioning applications. There may be times when this type of technology is not available or inconvenient to use, and additionally, some members of this population may prefer to watch the face of the talker for non-verbal cues (e.g., facial expressions that convey a range of emotions) that are lost in the captioning process. With the proposed tactual aid to lipreading, the user has access to a more complete and richer version of the spoken message. Thus, it is important to continue to develop tactual aids for individuals with profound hearing impairment for stand-alone use or as a supplement to hearing aids, cochlear implants, or captioning. A tactile aid to lipreading would be of significant benefit to the quality of life and well-being of millions of people with severe to profound hearing loss.

The TActile Phonemic Sleeve (TAPS) was recently developed for speech transmission through touch alone. Training and testing data from more than 100 individuals show that English speakers can learn to use TAPS within hours of training, and the best users acquire English words at a rate of 1 word per minute with a vocabulary size up to 500 words (essentially open vocabulary) [13, 14, 16]. The present research is aimed at a pared-down version of TAPS that supplements lipreading based on a phonemic coding scheme customized for the viseme groups of an individual deaf user of the device. In this paper we describe the design of the tactile aid to lipreading, and report on experiments conducted with one deaf participant to measure consonant recognition through lipreading alone and in combination with the tactile aid.

2   Methods

The experiments reported here were conducted under a protocol approved by the Internal Review Board (IRB) of MIT, through which the participant provided informed consent.

2.1   Consonant Confusion Patterns with Lipreading only

The first step in this project was to determine the consonant confusion patterns through lipreading alone of the deaf individual for whom the tactile aid was being designed. This participant (the second author of this paper) is an adult male who became profoundly deaf in early childhood. He is a non-native speaker of English whose first language is Russian. He does not use a hearing aid or cochlear implant, but has had previous experience with other tactile aids to lipreading (see [1]).

In the current study, the participant's ability to identify consonants in the initial position of consonant-vowel (CV) syllables through lipreading alone was examined using materials from the STeVi speech corpus of English.[1] The test syllables consisted of audio-visual recordings of 22 consonants (/p t k b d g f θ s ʃ v ð z ʒ tʃ dʒ m n r w l j/) with the vowels /i ɑ u/ produced by each of four talkers (2 M and 2 F) in the carrier phrase "You will mark [CV] please." Identification tests were conducted on each talker separately using a one-interval, 22-alternative forced-choice procedure. The experiment was controlled by a Matlab program (based on the AFC software developed by [3]) running on a desktop computer. The stimuli were presented over a computer monitor and the participant's task was to use a computer mouse to select a response from an orthographic display of the 22 stimuli that appeared after the stimulus had been presented. Each run consisted of 66 trials using random presentation without replacement of the syllables produced by a given talker. Trial-by-trial, correct-answer feedback was provided on the first run for each talker. The subsequent five runs, which employed a different repetition of the syllables, were conducted without feedback. Across the four talkers, 1320 test trials were obtained and used to construct a stimulus-response confusion matrix for data analysis summarized below.

Overall percent-correct score across talkers was 31.94% with overall information transmission of 2.031 bits. A hierarchical clustering analysis (performed in Matlab using a city-block distance measure and average linkage) yielded a dendritic tree with the following seven consonant clusters: /p b m/, /f v/, /θ ð/, /s z t d/, /ʃ ʒ tʃ dʒ/, /k g n j l/ and /r w/. These results are similar to those obtained in lipreading studies with native English speakers (see [9]), and were used to guide the development of the phonemic-based tactile aid to lipreading described below in Sect. 2.2.

2.2 Tactile Coding of Consonants to Supplement Lipreading

Our strategy in the design of a tactile code was to create tactile signals that would permit a lipreader to distinguish among the phonemes within each of the seven viseme groups identified above. The phonemes within each viseme group are assigned different tactile codes. By watching the face of the talker and attending to the tactile cue, the lipreader will be provided with sufficient information to distinguish among sounds that are highly confused through lipreading alone.

Description of Tactile Device. The tactile codes are presented through a 7-channel tactile device applied to the forearm and thenar eminence (see photo in Fig. 1). This device is a simplified version of the 24-channel phonemic-based

---

[1] (https://www.sens.com/products/stevi-speech-test-video-corpus/).

Fig. 1. Layout of tactors for the 7-channel tactile aid to lipreading.

tactile aid described by [14], using similar hardware, software, and principles for the selection of tactile codes. The actuators are wide-band tactors (Tectonic Elements, Model TEAX13C02-8/RH, Part #297–214, sourced from Parts Express International, Inc.) measuring 30 mm in diameter and 2 mm in thickness. Seven channels of a 24-channel USB audio device (MOTU, model 24Ao, Cambridge, MA) were used to deliver audio waveforms to each of the tactors through custom-built audio amplifiers. Matlab programs running on a desktop computer were used to generate waveforms to drive each tactor independently and synchronously with an associated video stimulus.

The user placed the left forearm on the vibrators palm side down such that the volar surface makes contact with the tactors labeled 2, 4, and 6, and the thenar eminence of the palm with tactor 7. The piece of material containing the tactors labeled 1, 3, and 5 was placed on top of the forearm and secured with strips of cloth that wrap around the arm and held in place with Velcro. Stimulus levels used in the speech experiments were established by first obtaining measurements of tactile thresholds at one tactor (the "reference" tactor labelled "3" in Fig. 1) for the frequencies used in the coding (60, 150, 250 Hz). A loudness-matching procedure was then used to adjust the level of each tactor such that its perceived strength was equal to that of the reference tactor for a 250-Hz signal presented at a level roughly 20 dB above threshold. These level adjustments in dB relative to maximum output for each tactor were applied to the other two stimulating frequencies (60 Hz and 150 Hz), based on data reported by [19] demonstrating similar loudness-growth contours across frequency.

Mapping of Phonemes to Tactile Display The device assumes real-time phoneme recognition at its front end. However, in order to remove the confound of phoneme-recognition accuracy with tactile code performance, the current study obtained perfect phoneme recognition using the non-real time Montreal Forced Aligner [7]. For consonants, each phoneme was assigned a tactile code whose duration was determined by the length of time it was recognized by the alignment scheme.

Table 1. Tactile codes for 22 phonemes, arranged by viseme group.

Phoneme	Tactor	Carrier (Hz)	30-Hz AM
/b/	5	250	No
/m/	5	250	Yes
/p/			
/v/	5	250	No
/f/			
/ð/	5	250	No
/θ/			
/d/	5	250	No
/t/			
/z/	1	250	Yes
/s/	1	250	No
/ʒ/	1	250	Yes
/ʃ/	1	250	No
/ʤ/	5	250	No
/ʧ/			
/r/	6	250	No
/w/	1	250	No
/l/	1	60	No
/j/	2	250	No
/n/	5	250	Yes
/g/	2	60	No
/k/			

The tactile codes are shown in Table 1 and are described in terms of the tactor that was used for stimulation (as numbered in Fig. 1), the carrier frequency in Hz, and the presence or absence of a 30-Hz amplitude modulation (AM) applied to the carrier frequency. A different tactile code is assigned to each phoneme within a viseme group. For example, for visemes /b m p/, /b/ is coded with a 250-Hz vibration at tactor 5, /m/ with a 250-Hz carrier with amplitude modulation at a rate 30 Hz at tactor 5, and /p/ is coded by the absence of a tactile signal. Among the full set of 22 consonants, codes were presented at four different locations (tactors labelled 1, 2, 5, and 6 in Fig. 1), used two different carrier frequencies (60 and 250 Hz), and were presented either with or without a 30-Hz amplitude modulation applied to the carrier frequency. The absence of a tactile signal was also used for coding, as shown for /p f t tʃ k/ in Table 1. Note that multiple phonemes can share the same tactile code (such as /m/ and /n/), as long as they belong to different viseme groups and thus are visibly different on the lips.

Table 2. Training results for each of the 11 stimulus sets.

Set	No. of phonemes	Stimulus set	Training with correct-answer feedback %-correct score			
			Run 1	Run 2	Run 3	Run 4
1	3	/p b m/	88.9	83.3	100	
2	4	/f v θ ð/	100			
3	7	Sets 1 + 2	90.5	100		
4	2	/r w/	100			
5	9	Sets 3 + 4	94.4			
6	4	/s z t d/	66.7	79.2	70.0	87.5
7	13	Sets 5 + 6	87.2			
8	4	/ʃ ʒ tʃ dʒ/	91.7			
9	17	Sets 7 + 8	84.1			
10	5	/l j n g k/	73.3	76.7	60.3	76.0
11	22	Sets 9 + 10	78.8			

The tactile stimulus codes were presented at a level of 30 dB SL relative to the threshold measured 250 Hz on tactor 3, and then applying the level adjustments for the remaining tactors for equal perceived strength, as described in Sect. 2.2 above.

In addition to the phoneme-specific codes, an envelope signal derived from an octave band of the acoustic speech signal with center frequency 500 Hz was used to drive a 150-Hz carrier at tactor 7 at a level of 30 dB SL.

2.3   Training and Testing with Tactile Aid as a Supplement to Lipreading

The participant received training in the use of the tactile aid in combination with lipreading, using the CV speech materials as described in Sect. 2.1 for the lipreading alone study. The participant was instructed to watch the lips of the talker and at the same time attend to the tactile code that was presented during a given stimulus presentation. The 22 consonants were grouped into sets for training (based primarily on viseme groups), and then gradually combined into larger groups over the course of the training. The eleven stimulus sets that were employed in the training are shown in the first three columns of Table 2. The sets are numbered from 1 through 11, as shown in the first column. The second and third columns provide the number of phonemes in the set and the identity of the phonemes, respectively. All stimuli introduced up to a given point in the training process are represented in sets 3, 5, 7, 9, and 11.

Training included the following steps for each stimulus set: The participant was shown a schematic diagram of the stimulus codes and felt them in isolation; the stimuli were presented in CV syllables in a fixed order; and closed-set identification tests were conducted with trial-by-trial feedback. When performance exceeded 80% correct or had leveled off, testing was conducted without feedback. The participant was given the option of repeating stimulus presentations before responding to focus on the integration of the tactile cue with lipreading. The identification tests were conducted as described in Sect. 2.1 adjusted to test only the stimuli in the set with the number of trials presented on the training and test runs updated to reflect the set. For stimulus sets with 2 to 13 phonemes (sets 1 through 8 and set 10), each run consisted of 6 randomized presentations of each consonant. For the larger stimulus sets (set 9 with 17 stimuli and set 11 with 22 stimuli), each run consisted of 3 randomized presentations of each consonant.

3   Consonant Recognition Results with Tactile Supplement

Results of training on the condition of lipreading with the tactile supplement are summarized in Table 2.

The %-correct score is shown after each run of trials with correct-answer feedback for the eleven sets of stimuli used in training. The number of training runs was dependent on performance as described above and thus varied across stimulus sets. Perfect performance of 100%-correct was achieved with training on the first 4 stimulus sets. For Sets 5 through 9, scores in the range of 84 to 94%-correct were achieved at the end of training. The most difficult viseme group was Set 10 where performance reached a plateau of 76% correct after 4 training runs. Performance for the full set of consonants in Set 11 reached 79% correct after one training run.

Following training with feedback, scores on each stimulus set were then obtained for tests conducted without the use of feedback. These scores were compared to scores obtained on each stimulus set for the condition of lipreading alone. In Fig. 2, %-correct scores are shown comparing lipreading alone with aided lipreading for each of the eleven stimulus sets, as defined in Table 2. The %-correct scores for lipreading alone is shown by the height of the blue bars, and the scores for the condition of lipreading combined with the tactile aid are shown by the height of the red bars. Performance with the tactile aid exceeded that with lipreading alone by at least 30% points for each of the sets. On Set 11, which included the full set of 22 consonants, an improvement of 31% points was obtained for the combined condition of lipreading plus the tactile aid (74.2%-correct) compared to lipreading alone (43.9%-correct).

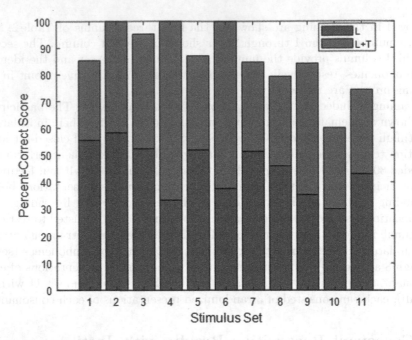

Fig. 2. Percent-correct scores for each of the 11 stimulus sets (as defined in Table 2) showing performance on lipreading alone (blue bars) and lipreading plus tactile aid (red bars). (Color figure online)

4   Discussion and Concluding Remarks

These preliminary studies with a phoneme-based tactile supplement to lipreading have shown promising results for improving the recognition of consonants for the deaf participant who received training with the aid. The results shown here for the benefits of the tactile aid compare favorably to those shown in previous evaluations of tactile aids (e.g., [4,20]). The results reported here, however, are limited to consonant recognition with one deaf participant. Further evaluations are necessary to include recognition of vowels as well as consonants, and to include a larger sample of persons with hearing impairment in the evaluations. Nonetheless, the results obtained in this preliminary evaluation are promising for continued work on the development of a wearable system.

Much of the previous work on the development of tactile aids has focused on a spectral-based approach to the processing and display of the acoustic speech signal. These devices employ spectral decomposition of the acoustic speech signal for presentation of different spectral bands to different places on the skin (e.g., see reviews in [5,11,12]). In contrast to spectral-based processing, recent work on tactile aids [e.g., [2,6,13,14,16–18,21]] has focused on a phoneme-based approach to encoding speech signals. This approach assumes the use of automatic speech recognition (ASR) at the front-end of the device for real-time recognition of phonemes. One important contrast between the spectral-based and phoneme-based approaches lies in the manner in which the inherent variability in speech tokens within and across talker is handled. In spectral-based displays, the burden of interpreting this variability falls in the tactile domain on the user of the device. In the phoneme-based approach, however, this task is accomplished by the ASR component, allowing the association of a specific tactile code to each phoneme. The use of an invariant code for each phoneme should be conducive to the process of integrating tactile signals with lipreading.

Further research on phoneme-based tactile supplements to lipreading is underway to extend the results of the preliminary study reported here. Ongoing work includes the design and evaluation of phoneme-based tactile codes for aided lipreading of vowels, as well as continued training and testing of deaf participants. Work is also planned for the development of a wearable version of this device. Such a tactile aid to lipreading would encompass real-time processing of the acoustic speech signal for extraction of features (such as voicing and nasality) that would then be encoded on a tactile array.

Acknowledgments. The authors wish to thank Dick Lyon, Pascal Getreuer, Artem Dementyev, and Malcolm Slaney of Google Research for their valuable discussions and feedback on this research.

References

1. Cholewiak, R.W., Sherrick, C.E.: Tracking skill of a deaf person with long-term tactile aid experience: a case study. J. Rehabil. Res. Dev. **23**(2), 20–26 (1986)
2. Dunkelberger, N., et al.: A multisensory approach to present phonemes as language through a wearable haptic device. IEEE Trans. Haptics **14**(1), 188–199 (2020)
3. Ewert, S.D.: AFC - A modular framework for running psychoacoustic experiments and computational perception models. In: Proceedings of the International Conference on Acoustics AIA-DAGA, pp. 1326–1329. Merano, Italy (2013)
4. Galvin, K.L., Ginis, J., Cowan, R.S., Blamey, P.J., Clark, G.M.: A comparison of a new prototype tickle talker^{TM} with the tactaid 7. Aust. N. Z. J. Audiol. **23**(1), 18–36 (2001)
5. Kappers, A.M., Plaisier, M.A.: Hands-free devices for displaying speech and language in the tactile modality-methods and approaches. IEEE Trans. Haptics **14**(3), 465–478 (2021). https://doi.org/10.1109/TOH.2021.3051737
6. Martinez, J.S., Tan, H.Z., Reed, C.M.: Improving tactile codes for increased speech communication rates in a phonemic-based tactile display. IEEE Trans. Haptics **14**(1), 200–211 (2020)
7. McAuliffe, M., Socolof, M., Mihuc, S., Wagner, M., Sonderegger, M.: Montreal forced aligner. Comput. Prog. Version 0.9.0 (2017). Accessed 17 Jan 2017. http://montrealcorpustools.github.io/Montreal-Forced-Aligner/
8. Mitchell, R.E.: How many deaf people are there in the United States? Estimates from the survey of income and program participation. J. Deaf Stud. Deaf Educ. **11**(1), 112–119 (2005). https://doi.org/10.1093/deafed/enj004
9. Owens, E., Blazek, B.: Visemes observed by hearing-impaired and normal-hearing adult viewers. J. Speech Lang. Hear. Res. **28**(3), 381–393 (1985)
10. Reed, C.M., Delhorne, L.A.: Current results of a field study of adult users of tactile aids. Semin. Hear. **16**(4), 305–315 (1995)

11. Reed, C.M., Durlach, N.I., Braida, L.D.: Research on tactile communication of speech: a review. ASHA Monogr. **20**, 1–23 (1982)
12. Reed, C.M., Durlach, N.I., Delhorne, L.A., Rabinowitz, W.M., Grant, K.W.: Research on tactual communication of speech: Ideas, issues, and findings. In: McGarr, N.S. (eds.) The Volta Review (Monograph entitled "Research on the Use of Sensory Aids for Hearing-Impaired People") (1989)
13. Reed, C.M., Tan, H.Z., Jiao, Y., Perez, Z.D., Wilson, E.C.: Identification of words and phrases through a phonemic-based haptic display: effects of inter-phoneme and inter-word interval durations. ACM Trans. Appl. Percept. **18**(3) (2021). https://doi.org/10.1145/3458725
14. Reed, C.M., et al.: A phonemic-based tactile display for speech communication. IEEE Trans. Haptics **12**(1), 2–17 (2019). https://doi.org/10.1109/TOH.2018.2861010
15. Ries, P.W.: Prevalence and characteristics of persons with hearing trouble, United States, 1990–91. National Center for Health Statistics. Series 10: Data from the National Health Survey No. 188 (1994)
16. Tan, H.Z., et al.: Acquisition of 500 English words through a TActile phonemic sleeve (TAPS). IEEE Trans. Haptics **13**(4), 745–760 (2020). https://doi.org/10.1109/TOH.2020.2973135
17. Turcott, R., et al.: Efficient evaluation of coding strategies for transcutaneous language communication. In: Prattichizzo, D., Shinoda, H., Tan, H.Z., Ruffaldi, E., Frisoli, A. (eds.) EuroHaptics 2018. LNCS, vol. 10894, pp. 600–611. Springer, Cham (2018). https://doi.org/10.1007/978-3-319-93399-3_51
18. de Vargas, M.F., Weill-Duflos, A., Cooperstock, J.R.: Haptic speech communication using stimuli evocative of phoneme production. In: 2019 IEEE World Haptics Conference (WHC 2019), pp. 610–615. IEEE (2019)
19. Verrillo, R.T., Fraioli, A.J., Smith, R.L.: Sensation magnitude of vibrotactile stimuli. Percept. Psychophysics **6**(6), 366–372 (1969). https://doi.org/10.3758/BF03212793
20. Weisenberger, J.M., Percy, M.E.: The transmission of phoneme-level information by multichannel tactile speech perception aids. Ear Hear. **16**(4), 392–406 (1995). https://doi.org/10.1097/00003446-199508000-00006
21. Zhao, S., Israr, A., Lau, F., Abnousi, F.: Coding tactile symbols for phonemic communication. In: Proceedings of the 2018 ACM CHI Conference on Human Factors in Computing Systems, pp. 1–13 (2018)

Perception

Effect of Subthreshold Vibration on the Perception of Electrovibration

Jagan K. Balasubramanian(✉) ⓘ, Rahul Kumar Ray ⓘ,
and Muniyandi Manivannan ⓘ

Touch Lab, Indian Institute of Technology Madras, Chennai, India
jagan.kb38@gmail.com, mani@iitm.ac.in

Abstract. Electrovibration is one of the methods by which users can perceive textures. Electrovibration along with vibrotactile stimulus can enhance texture perception. Several studies have already combined electrovibration and vibrotactile stimuli before, however at threshold or suprathreshold. Multi-modal stimuli at threshold had been reported to exhibit tactile masking inherently. Effect of stimuli at subthreshold and the tactile masking have been missing in the literature. In the current study, a psychophysical experiment was conducted to investigate the effect of subthreshold vibrotactile stimulus (SVS) on the perception of electrovibration. The results from the experiment indicate a reduction of electrovibration threshold by 28.52% at 90% SVS and 16.19% at 80% SVS. The 90% and 80% SVS are vibrotactile input at 90% and 80% of the absolute vibrotactile threshold. The experiment was conducted over a range of frequencies (20−320 Hz) for electrovibration, and the vibrotactile stimulus was maintained 235 Hz. The perception of the combined stimuli was evaluated in a separate experiment using the Likert's scale. The results showed that the sensation of electrovibration is dominating at 80% SVS than 90% SVS. The reduction in threshold of electrovibration (EVT) with SVS indicates the perception of electrovibration increased, and the effect of tactile masking was absent under subthreshold conditions. The study provides significant insights toward developing a texture rendering algorithm based on electrovibration and vibrotactile stimuli.

Keywords: Electrovibration · Vibrotactile · Subthreshold

1 Introduction

Touch-enabled devices such as Smartphones, tablets, notebooks, and kiosks are becoming increasingly popular.These devices with surface haptics can display textures along with graphics for enhancing immersion. The Addition of textures to the touch screens enables users to perceive the objects tactually along with the visual information in the various applications: e-commerce, education, user interfaces, refreshable braille, and aids for visually challenged [2].

Surface haptics through electrovibration attracted many researchers recently in which electrostatic friction between the finger and the surface was generated

© The Author(s), under exclusive license to Springer Nature Switzerland AG 2022
C. Saitis et al. (Eds.): HAID 2022, LNCS 13417, pp. 37–47, 2022.
https://doi.org/10.1007/978-3-031-15019-7_4

to render textures. The frictional force stimulates the mechanoreceptors such as Meissner's corpuscles, Merkel, Pacinian corpuscles, and Ruffini corpuscles, located beneath the skin. The Pacinian channel is primarily stimulated by electrovibration [17]. The electrostatic friction is generated due to the movement of fingers over a dielectric coated conductor supplied with a high-voltage alternating current signal [3]. Textures generated through electrovibration can be perceived better in the presence of multi modal stimuli [15, 18].

Several studies had been conducted on the effects of multi-modal stimuli on the perception of the base stimulus. Recent studies by Ray et al. [14] used SVS to reduce the threshold for electrotactile displays by 3–5% at 90% SVS and by 13–17% with background thermal stimulation [13]. In, electrotactile and thermal stimulation the nerve endings are activated directly by the passing of electric current whereas in electrovibration the mechanoreceptors are activated with the electrostatic forces between surface and the fingers [16]. With the reduction in threshold of electrotactile the authors were able to reduce the chance of the users to feel unpleasant shock sensation. Moreover the authors were also able to eliminate the effect of tactile masking. However the 3–5% reduction in threshold of electrotactile [14] is lower than the just noticeable difference (JND) of electrotactile stimulus which is 16% [6] and hence might not be perceivable. The use thermal actuators in the study [13] have low refresh rate and take long time to achieve the desired temperature. Semin Ryu et al. [15] studied the influence of vibrotactile stimulus with electrovibration. This study was conducted with the stimuli at threshold and supra-threshold conditions. The results from this study indicated that the combination of vibrotactile stimulus and electrovibration increased the EVT, resulting in tactile masking.

Vibrotactile stimulus invokes the perception of vibration by activating the mechanoreceptors and also can be used to generate textures on surfaces. Vibrotactile actuators are the most common tactile feedback systems, such as smartphones, tablets, and smartwatches. Eccentric Rotating Mass (ERMs) and Linear resonance actuators (LRAs) are commonly used vibrotactile actuators. ERMs and LRAs are both low-power actuators; however, due to the mass's inertia, ERMs have high startup and stop times. LRAs, on the other hand, can produce more complex shapes and has a cleaner vibrational profile [2, 5]. LRAs are generally more affordable and compact devices that do not require specialized hardware to actuate them [5]. In the current study, LRAs provide vibrotactile stimulus at subthreshold. LRAs are narrow band devices, and, for the current study, they were tuned 235 Hz since Pacinian corpuscles are resonant at that frequency [7, 16]. The study could have been conducted with a different frequency; however, as most devices are tuned at this frequency of peak sensitivity, 235 Hz was chosen for our study as well.

The multi-modal stimuli of electrovibration and vibrotactile at sub threshold is not studied in the literature. Previous studies had shown the multi-modal stimuli at supra-threshold and have reported tactile masking of electrovibration by vibrotactile stimulus. Tactile masking reduces the user's perception by increasing the EVT by vibrotactile stimulus. The current study investigates the effect of SVS on the perception of electrovibration and also finds whether the masking effect is present under subthreshold conditions. The psychophysical study measured EVT at 90% and 80% SVS, respectively, with frequencies ranging 20 Hz to 320 Hz. 90% and 80% SVS corresponds to vibrotactile input at 90% and 80% of the absolute vibrotactile threshold of the subject. The perception was evaluated on Likert's scale.

2   Experiment Protocol and Methodology

A psychophysical experiment was performed to measure the absolute EVT, threshold of vibrotactile stimuli and their combinations. A signal generator and current amplifier were used for actuating LRA, while the electrovibration used a high voltage source, a high voltage amplifier, and a signal generator as shown in Fig. 1.

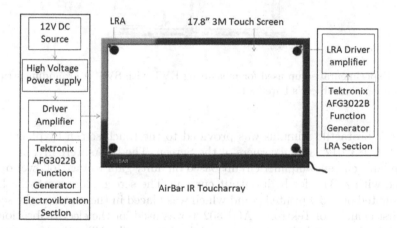

Fig. 1. Block diagram of the electrovibration and vibrotactile setup. Four LRAs are placed on the corners of the touchscreen to provide subthreshold vibrotactile stimulus.

2.1   Experimental Setup

A setup was designed to actuate both LRA and electrovibration display. A 17.8" capacitive touch screen (17-9241-225) from 3M was used to generate the surface textures using electrovibration. An IR touch screen was used to monitor the speed of finger movement. A high voltage power supply (rating of 1 KV at 2 mA) powered a custom made amplifier circuit to provide electrovibration stimulus. The input wave-forms for the amplifier were generated using a function generator (Tektronix AGF3022b). The amplitude of the power supply was restricted to 250 V_{pp} and 600 µA to ensure the safety of users.

Vardar *et al.* [17] had reported that electrovibration with pulse wave were better perceived than sinusoidal signals. Therefore, a pulse signal was chosen for the experiment which was maintained at 50% duty cycle with varying amplitude and frequency. The experiment was performed for a frequency range 20 Hz to 320 Hz, with 3dB difference between two consecutive frequencies (20, 40, 80, 160, 320 Hz). This method was chosen because of linear relation between logarithmic frequencies and perception, and it had previously been shown by Ray et al. [14]. The amplitude of the signal was adjusted so as to measure the EVT.

Fig. 2. Experimental setup used for measuring EVT with SVS. A grounding strip was placed under the subject's bare foot.

The Vibrotactile stimulus was provided to the touch screen by placing four LRAs "VG0832012" at the corners of the Screen. The LRAs were driven using a custom built current amplifier circuit based on unity gain voltage follower opamp buffered with a BJT for high output current. The screen along with the LRAs was mounted on a 3D printed stand which was placed in the centre of the screen. The First channel of Tektronix AGF3022b was used for the electrovibration display while the second channel was used for LRAs. The Vibration frequency of LRAs was maintained constant 235 Hz (resonant frequency of LRA). Since electrovibration stimulus had a pulse wave input, the LRAs were also provided with the same input. Compared to other types of vibrotactile actuators, LRAs had no problem in replicating the pulse wave. An optical Non-Contact Displacement Transducer (optoNCDT 2300) was used to measure the displacement of the LRAs. The input to the LRAs was 235 Hz pulse wave with 50% duty cycle which is in coherent with opto-NCDT reading.

2.2 Subjects

Fifteen graduate subjects from the institute (11 males and 4 females) with an age of 28 ± 4, were selected for the current study. To avoid the effects of dead skin cells, subjects washed and subsequently dried their hands before the experiment. Subjects used the index finger of the dominant hand to actively scroll the screen with a speed of 0.5 to 1 m/s (measured and showed on the screen) and follow a moving block to maintain the constant speed during the whole experiment [9]. 5 to 6 sample trails were given before the experiment to acquaint the subjects with electrovibration and vibrotactile stimuli. The trails were for short duration and was conducted 15 min before the experiment to prevent the subjects from getting biased. Subjects were asked to wear noise cancelling headphones and white noise was played on the headphones to avoid the experimental bias from the audio noise of vibrotactile stimulus and environmental noise. The setup used for the experiment is shown in Fig. 2.

2.3   Experimental Procedure

A psychophysical experiment was conducted to measure the EVT with and without SVS. The Staircase method was used to measure the absolute EVT and vibrotactile perception threshold (VPT). The Staircase method was repeated thrice and the average value was taken as The threshold at any chosen frequency. We selected this adaptive technique due to its efficiency in determining the subject's threshold [7].

The experiment comprises four stages for measuring the absolute thresholds for electrovibration and vibrotactile stimulation alone and in the subthreshold combinations: 1) VPT alone, 2) EVT alone, 3) EVT at 90% SVS, and 4) EVT at 80 %SVS.

VPT was measured in the first stage keeping the electrovibration off. A pulse signal from the signal generator was applied to the LRAs 235 Hz and a duty cycle of 50%. The amplitude of the signal was increased from 1 mV with a step size of 5mV till the subjects reported as "Yes" and perceived the vibration and then the amplitude of stimulus was decreased in smaller steps (1 mV) till they reported as "No" for the absence of a stimulus. This 1 up 1 down technique estimates the threshold at the 50% point on a psychometric function. The method was repeated one more time till they reported the presence of stimulus as "Yes". The amplitudes at these three "yes", "No", and "yes" were averaged to measure the VPT. The subthreshold values were calculated by taking the 90% and 80% of VPT. The average value was calculated after 3 transition points to keep the experiment short so that subjects don't feel any fatigue [9].

Absolute EVT was measured in the second stage keeping the vibrotactile stimulus off. The threshold was measured using staircase method similar to the first stage at five different frequencies (20, 40, 80, 160, and 320 Hz), where the only difference was 3 V step size in the voltage increment and 1 V in the decrement. In the third stage and fourth stage, EVT was measured with SVS at 90% and 80% of the VPT measured in the first stage, respectively. Subjects rated the perception based on Likert's scale (between one to five) to quantitatively analyze the perception of combined stimulus. The Likert's scale for this psychophysical study is explained as follows, where '1' represents pure vibrotactile, '2' represents the domination of vibrotactile over electrovibration, '3' represents the equality of both, '4' represents the domination of electrovibration over vibrotactile and '5' represents pure electrovibration. Subjects rated the perception of combined stimuli on Likert's scale in the third and fourth stages. The experiments were not conducted for higher SVS as the setup could not achieve enough trial points to calculate the threshold through the staircase method. Similarly, the SVS was not reduced beyond 80% since the duration of the experiment was limited to avoid experimental fatigue in participants.

3   Results

The objective of the current study was to analyze the effect of SVS on perception of electrovibration.

The average VPT measured in terms of displacement in 'μm' for fifteen subjects in the first stage of the experiment was 0.68 μm 235 Hz with a median value of 0.664 μm. The maximum and minimum VPT of any subject was 0.916 μm and 0.428μm respectively.

Figure 3a shows the normalized EVT (EVTn) plotted against the frequency. The amplitude of EVT is normalized with the average EVT 20 Hz. The plot has three curves: EV, EV-I and EV-II representing value of EVTn at stage-2, 90% SVS and 80% SVS respectively. The curves in Fig. 3a follow a V-shaped trend in the tuning curve. The maximum EVT in the second stage for any subject was 80 V. Percentage reduction in EVT (Average of fifteen subjects) with the frequency of electrovibration is plotted in Fig. 3b. Since both the curves follow a zigzag pattern, we can infer that reduction was frequency independent. When the vibrotactile stimulus was maintained at 90% subthreshold the maximum percentage reduction in EVT was 32.4% with an average of 28.52%. Similarly When vibrotactile stimulus was at 80%, 19.32% maximum with an average reduction of 16.19% for the average of fifteen subjects. In both the subthreshold conditions, the percentage reduction in EVT is lowest 80 Hz in EV-II and 320 Hz in EV-I.

Likert's scale values for third (90% SVS) and fourth (80% SVS) stages are represented by L-I and L-II plots as shown in Fig. 4. The figure showed that L-I is closer to '3', indicating that the subjects were unable to determine the dominant stimulus. In contrast, L-II is closer to '5', which represents the dominance of electrovibration.

To statistically test the significant difference among the values of EV, EV-I, and EV-II, we conducted a two-way factorial ANOVA test without replication. The statistical test was conducted for average threshold of all subjects and individual subjects as well. Results from the statistical tests for the average of 15 subjects are shown in Table 1. In the Anova test, two null hypotheses are

Table 1. Statistical Analysis: Two way factorial ANOVA test between EV, EV-I and EV-II. Here VTf and VTs are variation in thresholds with frequencies and different levels of subthreshold stimuli respectively.

Source of variation	F	p-value	$F_{critical}$
VTf	75.83	$9.83 * 10^{-6}$	3.84
VTs	67.44	$1.29 * 10^{-5}$	4.46

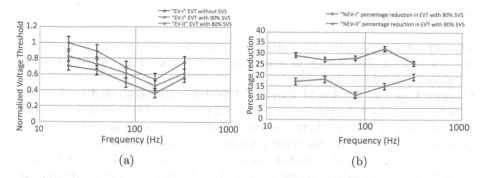

Fig. 3. (a) Normalized average EVT (Electrovibration threshold) of fifteen subjects plotted over frequency, the maximum average EVT 20 Hz was taken to normalize the curves. EV (blue) represents EVT in the absence of vibrotactile stimulus, EV-I (orange) represents EVT with 90% SVS (Subthreshold vibrotactile stimulus) and EV-II (grey) represents the EVT with 80% SVS (b) Percentage reduction in EVT is plotted over frequency for the average of fifteen subjects. %EV-I (blue) represents the percentage reduction in EVT when the SVS was at 90% and %EV-II (orange) represents the percentage reduction in EVT when the SVS was at 80% SVS (orange).

tested for variation of thresholds with the frequency (VTf) and the variation of the threshold with different levels of subthreshold stimuli (VTs). According to Table 1, F value is higher than F-critical for both the VTf and VTs and the p-values are smaller than 0.05 for both the VTf and VTs, which infers that the null hypothesis for both the rows and columns can be rejected. In other words, there is a significant statistical difference among the values of EV, EV-I, and EV-II.

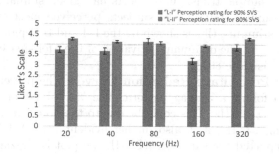

Fig. 4. Perception characterization is plotted for every frequency with 90% SVS (L-I) and 80% SVS (L-II). Rating of '1' represents pure vibrotactile sensation and Rating '5' represents pure electrovibration sensation. (Color figure online)

4   Discussion

The current study explored the effects of introducing SVS to the perception of electrovibration. The change in perception was measured as the change in the EVT by psychophysical study.

Observation of Threhsold Curves: The study was conducted for 90% and 80% SVS, and the reduction in EVT was 28.52% and 16.19% respectively, which is higher than the JND of electrovibration, that is 7.77% as reported by Bau *et al.* [3], this indicates that the users will perceive the combination of the stimuli. Due to the combination of Vibrotactile and electrovibration stimuli, it was essential to investigate their effects on each other. We observed from our experimental results that EVT reduces with the SVS. Since both modalities (electrovibration and vibrotactile) actuates mechanoreceptors through stretch-activated ion channels (SAICS), specially Pacinian, depending upon the frequency of stimuli as reported in the previous studies [11,12,16], appropriate frequency for the experiment was chosen 20 Hz 320 Hz for electrovibration 235 Hz for vibrotactile stimulus, since Pacinian is resonant 235 Hz. kajimoto *et al.* reported that [10] the response of mechanoreceptors (Meissner, Merkel, and Ruffini) other than Pacinian and Meissner corpuscle are limited 30 Hz. So, all the frequencies 20 Hz would activate Pacinian alone for both stimuli. Therefore, the presence of cross-coupling between both modalities is certain. This can be observed in the V-shaped curve as it follows the human detection threshold curve for touch as mentioned by Gescheider [7].

Observation of Likert's Scale: The Likert's scale reading Fig. 4 indicates that the subjects felt overall dominance of electrovibration when SVS was present; this is indicated the slight difference between the L-I and L-II. However, 80% SVS is far lower than absolute VPT; hence the subjects felt that the electrovibration is more prominent compared to 90% SVS, which is slightly lower than absolute VPT. During the sample trials, the subjects had given similar ratings for the combination of stimuli. A80 Hz, the subjects perceived electrovibration more than vibrotactile stimulus; this is shown by the L-I and L-II plots in Fig. 4. This reason could be due to the dominant activation of the Meissner corpuscle whose natural frequency is close 80 Hz.

Observation of Percentage Reduction Curves: The percentage reduction curves in Fig. 3b follow a zig-zag pattern. The %EV-I is constant across all frequencies, peaking 160 Hz. This could be due to the dominance of vibrotactile stimulus vibrating 235 Hz; it is also further evident from L-I in Fig. 4 where the users have reported the same. In %EV-II, the plot is zig-zag; this could be due to the dominance of electrovibration as shown in L-I and L-II 80 Hz. The outliers 80 Hz in both plots, Fig. 4 and 3b, may be different when different LRA frequencies and depend on the finger's biomechanics. However, this effect is a matter of future study.

Dependence on Finger Motion: The VPT depends on the state of the finger, whether it is stationary or moving. When the finger was stationary, the threshold was lower compared to a moving finger. It is verified by a pilot study on five subjects to investigate the effect of finger movements on the threshold. The study showed that the VPT is significantly lower in static finger compared to finger under motion. However, the variation in motion did not alter the VPT. Furthermore, the 5 to 6 sample trails after the previous pilot study enabled the subjects to identify the presence of the dominant stimulus during the experiment. **Applied Pressure:** Finger pressure impacts the perception of electrovibration. In the current study, we instructed the participants to explore the screen with a touch-like interaction (without applying force or body weight). Zophoniasson *et al.* [18] conducted a study on the applied forces and tactile perception thresholds for electrovibration. The results from their psychophysical studies concluded that their isn't any effect of applied force on the threshold for lower frequencies (up 160 Hz) however, threshold increases for higher frequencies with the application of force. In the current study, the frequency for electrovibration stimuli 20 Hz, 40 Hz, 80 Hz, 160 Hz 320 Hz. Therefore, 320 Hz, there is a possibility of effects of applied force on the threshold and at all the other frequencies, the effects of applied force would be negligible.

Tactile Masking: When multi-modal stimuli are applied, there is a probability of threshold increment for one of the stimuli in the presence of another stimulus, this phenomenon is known as tactile masking. Vardar *et al.* [16] have reported that tactile masking in sinusoidal electrovibration bursts (125 Hz) by providing masking signals using noise bursts. Ryu *et al.* and Jamalzadeh *et al.* [8,15] have reported that EVT increased with the increase in the intensity of the vibro-tactile stimulus at suprathreshold. However, in the current study the reduction in the EVT with SVS suggests that tactile masking absent under subthreshold conditions.

Relevance to Steven's Power Factor. Steven's power factor relates the perception intensity to the stimulus intensity. The current study used two tactile stimuli of different modalities and therefore with different Steven's power factor: 0.93 for vibrotactile and 0.492 for electrovibration as reported by Aghilone *et al.* and Chen *et al.* in their works [1] and [4], respectively. Steven's power factor for both of the tactile stimuli are less than unity, the perception response with the stimulus intensity is a rapid rise in the lower range of frequency. Reduction in the EVT makes the perception faster compared to vibrotactile which has Steven's power factor closer to unity. Therefore when the combination of the stimulus was perceptually measured by participants, the response was inclined towards electrovibration dominance as mentioned in the Likert's scale values in Fig. 4.

5 Conclusion and Future Works

The current study explored the effects of introducing SVS to the perception of electrovibration. We have found a 28.52% reduction with 90% SVS and 16.19% reduction with 80% SVS, which is higher than the JND of electrovibration and will be definitely perceived by the users. The reduction in EVT suggests that tactile masking was absent with SVS and the perception of electrovibration improved with SVS. The combined stimuli were perceptually measured by subjects and it was found that the perception was dominant towards electrovibration when SVS was at 80% compared 90% SVS, respectively. The vibrotactile stimulus was actuated only 235 Hz in the current study, it would be insightful to repeat the study at other frequencies. We did not measure the applied force to the screen in the current study and asked user to maintain a similar force. The future scope of the current study includes the different combinations of modalities for the threshold reduction. In the current study, it was found that the percentage reduction curve didn't follow the V-shaped trend, the reason for this can be investigated in future studies. This study provides significant insights to develop texture rendering algorithm with the combination of electrovibration and vibrotactile sensation. The algorithm can render textures based on electrovibration alone at 80% SVS with the added advantage of reduced electrovibration threshold. At 90% SVS the algorithm can render textures with the combination of both the stimuli.

References

1. Aghilone, G., Cavacece, M.: Evaluation of stevens' power law exponents for whole-body vibration by psychophysical methods. Prog. Vib. Acoust. **3**, 1–20 (2015). https://doi.org/10.12866/J.PIVAA.2015.01.01
2. Basdogan, C., Giraud, F., Levesque, V., Choi, S.: A review of surface haptics: enabling tactile effects on touch surfaces. IEEE Trans. Haptics **13**(3), 450–470 (2020). https://doi.org/10.1109/TOH.2020.2990712
3. Bau, O., Poupyrev, I., Israr, A., Harrison, C.: Teslatouch: electrovibration for touch surfaces. In: Proceedings of the 23nd annual ACM Symposium on User Interface Software and Technology, pp. 283–292, October 2010. https://doi.org/10.1145/1866029.1866074
4. Chen, Y., Qiu, W., Wang, X., Zhang, M.: Tactile rendering of fabric textures based on texture recognition. In: 2019 IEEE THE 2nd International Conference on Micro/Nano Sensors for AI, Healthcare, and Robotics (NSENS), pp. 87–91. IEEE (2019)
5. Choi, S., Kuchenbecker, K.J.: Vibrotactile display: Perception, technology, and applications. Proc. IEEE **101**(9), 2093–2104 (2013). https://doi.org/10.1109/JPROC.2012.2221071
6. Dideriksen, J., Markovic, M., Lemling, S., Farina, D., Dosen, S.: Electrotactile and vibrotactile feedback enable similar performance in psychometric tests and closed-loop control. IEEE Trans. Haptics **15**(1), 222–231 (2021)
7. Gescheider, G.A.: Psychophysics: the Fundamentals. Psychology Press, London (2013)
8. Jamalzadeh, M., Güçlü, B., Vardar, Y., Basdogan, C.: Effect of remote masking on detection of electrovibration. In: 2019 IEEE World Haptics Conference (WHC), pp. 229–234. IEEE (2019)
9. Jones, L.A., Tan, H.Z.: Application of psychophysical techniques to haptic research. IEEE Trans. Haptics **6**(3), 268–284 (2012)
10. Kajimoto, H., Kawakami, N., Maeda, T., Tachi, S.: Electro-tactile display with tactile primary color approach. The University of Tokyo, Graduate School of Information and Technology (2004)
11. Madhan Kumar, V., Sadanand, V., Manivannan, M.: Computational model of a Pacinian corpuscle for hybrid-stimuli: spike-rate and threshold characteristics. In:

Manocha, A.K., Jain, S., Singh, M., Paul, S. (eds.) Computational Intelligence in Healthcare. HIS, pp. 379–396. Springer, Cham (2021). https://doi.org/10.1007/978-3-030-68723-6_21

12. Osgouei, R.H.: Electrostatic friction displays to enhance touchscreen experience. In: Xiao, D., Sankaran, K. (eds.) Modern Applications of Electrostatics and Dielectrics, chap. 4. IntechOpen, Rijeka (2020). https://doi.org/10.5772/intechopen.91056

13. Ray, R.K., Manivannan, M.: Reduction of electrotactile perception threshold using background thermal stimulation. In: Ahram, T., Taiar, R. (eds.) IHIET 2021. LNNS, vol. 319, pp. 331–338. Springer, Cham (2022). https://doi.org/10.1007/978-3-030-85540-6_42

14. Ray, R.K., Patel, P., Manivannan, M.: Reduction of electrotactile perception threshold using subthreshold vibrotactile stimuli. Displays, p. 102056 (2021)

15. Ryu, S., Pyo, D., Lim, S.C., Kwon, D.S.: Mechanical vibration influences the perception of electrovibration. Sci. Rep. 8(1), 1–10 (2018)

16. Vardar, Y., Güçlü, B., Basdogan, C.: Tactile masking by electrovibration. IEEE Trans. Haptics 11(4), 623–635 (2018)

17. Vardar, Y., Güçlü, B., Basdogan, C.: Effect of waveform on tactile perception by electrovibration displayed on touch screens. IEEE Trans. Haptics 10(4), 488–499 (2017). https://doi.org/10.1109/TOH.2017.2704603

18. Zophoniasson, H., Bolzmacher, C., Anastassova, M., Hafez, M.: Electrovibration: influence of the applied force on tactile perception thresholds. In: 2017 Zooming Innovation in Consumer Electronics International Conference (ZINC), pp. 70–73 (2017). https://doi.org/10.1109/ZINC.2017.7968666

Incorporating Thermal Feedback in Cutaneous Displays: Reconciling Temporal and Spatial Disparities

Lynette A. Jones[1]([⊠]) and Hsin-Ni Ho[2]

[1] Department of Mechanical Engineering, Massachusetts Institute of Technology,
Cambridge, MA 02139, USA
ljones@MIT.edu
[2] Faculty of Design, Kyushu University, Fukuoka, Japan
hohsinni@design.kyushu-u.ac.jp

Abstract. There are fundamental differences between the tactile and thermal sensory systems that must be accommodated when designing multisensory cutaneous displays for use in virtual or teleoperated robotic environments. In this review we highlight the marked temporal and spatial differences between the senses of cold and warmth as revealed in psychophysical experiments. Cold and warmth are distinct senses with marked differences in the time taken to respond to stimulation and in their temporal filtering processes. Such variations must be taken into account when time-varying profiles of thermal stimulation are delivered to the skin concurrent with tactile stimulation since the resulting sensations will not be perceived on the same time scale. Although it is often reported that the thermal senses are markedly inferior to the sense of touch with respect to their spatial acuity, it is also clear that there is considerable variability across the body in the accuracy with which thermal stimuli can be localized. The distal to proximal gradient in thermal acuity suggests that locations other than the palmar surface of the hand are better suited for displaying thermal cues, in contrast to the situation for tactile inputs. As was noted for temporal processes, there are differences between localizing warmth and cold stimuli, with localization being superior for cold. These properties provide benchmarks that can be used in designing thermal and multisensory displays.

Keywords: Cutaneous sensing · Multisensory · Thermal displays

1 Introduction

Multisensory displays that present visual and auditory cues to users have been extensively investigated. There is also a substantial body of research that has evaluated how the tactile sense interacts with visual and auditory processes and the conditions under which it provides added benefit to such interactions [1]. The latter research has highlighted the contribution of tactile inputs as part of multisensory interfaces where they complement the information provided by other sensory channels. One function that can be supported by adding tactile cues to an interface is an increased bandwidth of information transfer in complex data-rich environments, where the visual and auditory channels have traditionally been heavily relied upon. In these applications, the sense of touch is being used to offload the visual and auditory modalities and to present information that would otherwise be delayed or not available at all.

Displays that optimize the information conveyed by stimulating the skin are of widespread interest due to the pervasiveness of mobile devices and wearable technologies, both of which rely excessively on vision for communication [2–4]. By combining vibration, pressure, and skin stretch in a single display the information provided to the user can be augmented and particular cues can be associated with specific types of tactile inputs. Although there are numerous studies of the visual and auditory senses that indicate that with increased dimensionality of a display there is an increase in the amount of information that can be received by the user [5], much less is known about multi-dimensional tactile displays. What has been studied has typically focused on static displays and information transfer rather than dynamic displays and the rate of information transfer.

Changes in skin temperature provide an additional signal that can be combined with tactile cues to create a multisensory cutaneous display. Early research on thermal displays focused on simulating the thermal cues associated with holding an object to determine if these cues could be used to assist in identifying its material composition [6, 7]. Results from this research demonstrated that users were able to identify the material composition of a variety of objects based on the output from these model-based thermal displays. User performance was determined to be comparable to that achieved with real materials [8, 9]. More recently, thermal displays have been evaluated in the context of enhancing user interactions with objects presented on digital media or in virtual environments, for example by changing skin temperature to convey emotional content [10, 11], to present scalar information that is mapped onto temperature [12] or to improve situational awareness in driving scenarios [13, 14]. These displays have also been used to create thermal icons [15] by analogy to tactile icons or tactons in the tactile domain. Thermal icons have been designed by varying the direction (warming or cooling), amplitude, spatial extent and duration of thermal stimulation. The contexts in which thermal icons have been evaluated include enhancing affective communication in human computer interactions [16], assisting in navigation by giving proximity cues [17], and providing prompts regarding the source and importance of incoming text messages on mobile devices [18]. The parameters of the thermal icons created for these experiments were based on data from pilot studies rather than being derived from models of the changes in skin temperature and resulting sensations associated with different thermal inputs.

To address this shortcoming, Singhal and Jones [19] used linear system identification techniques to develop a dynamic model of the changes in skin temperature as a function of thermal input signals. The model could predict changes in skin temperature from unrelated experiments involving thermal icons. Further work by Ho et al. [20] using linear systems theory modelled the temporal profile of the resulting sensation as a function of the waveform of the thermal input. This model predicted the response delay and the distortion in the temporal profile of the resulting sensation when perceiving dynamic thermal inputs. These two models provide the foundation for a model-based approach to creating thermal icons.

The combination of tactile and thermal inputs in multi-sensory cutaneous displays has the potential to increase the sense of realism and immersion in virtual and augmented reality environments and enhance the bandwidth available for skin-based communication [10, 21, 22]. For multisensory feedback to be effectively implemented it is important to understand the fundamental properties of the tactile and thermal sensory systems, and in particular how their temporal and spatial features differ. In this paper we provide an overview of thermal perceptual processes from the perspective of designing cutaneous displays that enhance object recognition or information transmission; the particular focus is on temporal and spatial processing. The findings presented are from research studies conducted over a number of years in which we have sought to characterize tactile and thermal perception as it relates to the design of thermo-haptic devices.

2   Temporal Processes

One of the challenges associated with presenting tactile and thermal cues concurrently is the profound difference between the senses in the time taken to process information. Reaction times for tactile stimuli are much faster than those for thermal stimuli which means that concurrent thermo-tactile stimulation will not necessarily be perceived as simultaneous. In addition, decreases in skin temperature signaled by cold thermoreceptors are responded to more rapidly than increases in skin temperature sensed by warm thermoreceptors. These variations in response times primarily reflect the conduction velocities of the peripheral afferent fibers with the Aβ fibers associated with tactile mechanoreceptors having conduction velocities of 35–75 m/s as compared to the conduction velocity of 5–15 m/s of the Aδ fibers from cold thermoreceptors and the 1–2 m/s of C fibers that innervate warm thermoreceptors [23, 24]. A further temporal factor to consider is the time course of the response of the skin to thermal stimulation. As illustrated in Fig. 1 below, when the skin is in contact with a Peltier-based thermal display there is a delay in its response to warming and cooling, and the gain is less than one due to its lower bandwidth [25].

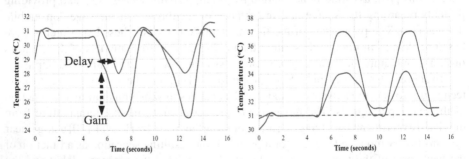

Fig. 1. Temperatures measured using thermistors mounted on a Peltier module (blue) and at two locations on the skin, one in contact with the thermal display (green) and one not in contact with the display (red). Redrawn and adapted from [25]. (Color figure online)

An additional consideration in thermal temporal processing is that humans perceive temporal information regarding warming and cooling differently due to the distinct temporal filtering properties of the senses of warmth and cold [20]. As demonstrated in Fig. 2A, the temporal impulse response function of the sense of cold has a shorter system delay and a larger transience factor than that of the sense of warmth. In other words, the sense of cold responds to a stimulus quicker, and the resulting sensation declines in a shorter time than the sense of warmth. This difference in the temporal filtering properties directly modulates the resulting sensations for dynamic warming and cooling stimulation. For example, the senses of warmth and cold have distinct sensations resulting from a full-cycle sinusoid stimulation (Fig. 2B) and a half-cycle sinusoid stimulation (Fig. 2C). The peak responses, that is the coolest or the warmest sensations, are delayed

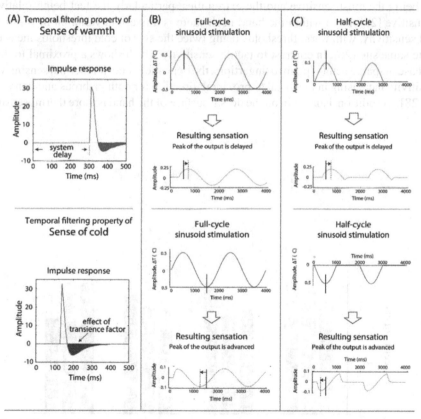

Fig. 2. Differences in temporal filtering properties of the senses of warmth and cold. The difference is demonstrated in the impulse responses of the warm and cold systems and the output responses to the full-cycle and half-cycle sinusoid stimulations. The vertical solid (dashed) lines represent the timing of the physical (perceptual) warm peak, and physical (perceptual) cold peak. Note that the gain is arbitrarily set to 1 in both systems, so the absolute values of the amplitude in the impulse responses and output responses are not informative, and the units are omitted. Attention should be paid to the relative change in amplitude across time. Redrawn and adapted from [20].

for the warming stimulation but advanced for the cooling stimulation. It is crucial to consider these differences in the temporal filtering properties of the senses of warmth and cold, especially when presenting tactile feedback with dynamic warming/cooling stimulation concurrently.

3 Spatial Processes

3.1 Pattern Recognition

With respect to the spatial properties of the thermal senses, the vast landscape of skin provides an extensive area for communication. As with the sense of touch, there are substantial variations in thermal sensitivity across the body with the cheeks and the lips being the most sensitive and the extremities, particularly the feet being relatively insensitive [26]. Even within the hand itself there is a five-fold variation in warm and cold sensitivity, with warm thresholds being twice the size of cold thresholds measured at the same site [26]. In contrast to tactile sensitivity which shows a proximal to distal increase in spatial acuity (palm to fingertips), the opposite occurs for thermal sensing with sensitivity increasing in the distal to proximal direction for both glabrous and hairy skin [27, 28]. In addition, hairy skin on the dorsal surface of the hand is more thermosensitive

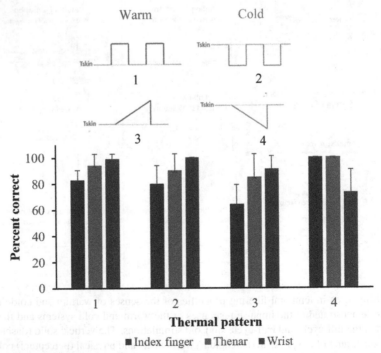

Fig. 3. Upper: Representative thermal patterns that varied in terms of the direction of temperature change (warming and cooling) and waveform. Lower: Percent correct score identifying the four thermal patterns at three sites on the arm. The group (N = 10) mean (standard deviation) responses are shown.

than glabrous skin, when evaluated in terms of warm and cold thresholds [29] or ratings of the magnitude of supra-threshold stimuli [30]. These variations in thermal sensitivity are also reflected in differences in the ability to identify thermal patterns.

In a series of studies, we compared the accuracy with which participants could identify thermal patterns that varied with respect to the magnitude and rate of change in temperature. Three sites were tested: the fingertips, the thenar eminence at the base of the thumb and the wrist. Participants identified the stimulus using a visual template of the thermal waveforms [19]. The objective of this work was to determine whether specific sites on the hand and arm would be optimal for mounting a thermal display due to their enhanced capacity to process thermal cues. As illustrated for a set of representative thermal stimuli shown in Fig. 3, patterns displayed on the thenar eminence or wrist were identified more consistently (92% and 91% correct respectively) than those displayed on the fingertips (82% correct) (Friedman's test, $p < 0.01$).

These findings indicate that variations in thermal sensitivity at different locations on the hand occur for all types of suprathreshold stimuli. In addition, there is consistent evidence across a broad range of studies of a distal to proximal progression in thermal acuity and overall perceptual performance. In the context of a multisensory cutaneous displays, it may be more efficacious to distribute tactile and thermal feedback across the hand and arm rather than co-locating them, for example by displaying tactile cues on the fingertips and thermal information more proximally on the wrist or forearm.

3.2 Localization

The ability to localize a stimulus in space is a fundamental feature of all sensory modalities and is particularly important when information from the external environment is mapped onto the body. Numerous studies have demonstrated that spatial information maps well on to the skin, particularly the torso and forearm, making the tactile sense the preferred medium for displays conveying cues related to orientation and navigation [31]. In contrast, the thermal senses are markedly inferior at localizing the site of thermal stimulation and at differentiating two thermal stimuli placed in close proximity. This is not surprising in that as homeothermic mammals, sensing the overall thermal state of the body is essential to regulating body temperature and so spatial summation across the skin surface is a critical feature for maintaining core temperature. It has been reported that low intensity warm stimuli presented 150 mm apart on the forearm are not perceived as distinct [32], although localization errors for warm stimuli are much smaller on the dorsal surface of the hand averaging 19 mm [33]. There do not appear to be any studies that have used an identical protocol to examine localization accuracy for warm and cold stimuli at the same location.

A direct comparison of the precision with which the location of cold and warm stimuli is perceived would provide insight into the underlying perceptual processes for the thermal senses and give a benchmark for determining the optimal density of thermal actuators in an array based on localization acuity. In a series of experiments, we have examined localization accuracy for warm and cold stimuli presented along the forearm using the setup depicted in Fig. 4. The display comprised three Peltier modules (22 mm long and 19 mm wide, and 3.8 mm thick) with a center-to-center distance of 75 mm between the modules. The contact area of each module was 418 mm^2. Ten participants (24–36 years) took part in each of the experiments.

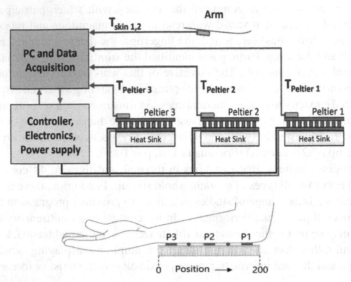

Fig. 4. Schematic diagram of the thermal display and its location on the forearm with three Peltier modules (P1–P3) mounted on heat sink and thermistors measuring the temperatures (T) of the modules and at two locations on the forearm (red dots in the lower diagram). (Color figure online)

Four thermal pulses 2 s in duration that either cooled (8 °C decrease) or warmed (6 °C increase) the skin were presented on the forearm. The rate of temperature change was 3 °C/s with an inter-stimulus interval of 4 s. The warm stimuli had a smaller absolute magnitude than the cold stimuli to ensure that they did not elicit pain. The first two stimuli were always delivered at the same location and the position of the other two pulses varied. The focus of the results presented here is on the perceived position of the first two stimuli that were delivered either near the elbow (P1) or the wrist (P3) as illustrated in Fig. 4. Participants were not informed about the specific locations of the stimuli and used a cursor to indicate the positions of the two stimuli on a visual representation of the forearm presented on a GUI on a computer screen. In order to avoid any adaptation, the arm in contact with the thermal display changed after every two trials. Each stimulus set was presented five times giving a total of 20 stimuli for each condition. The cold and warm stimuli were presented on different days.

The perceived location of the two stimuli were digitized using the Image Processing Toolbox in MATLAB (Mathworks, Inc.) with the distance being measured from the wrist as shown in Fig. 4. A format originally devised by Goldreich [34] and employed in studies of thermal illusions [35] was used to conceptualize the actual and perceived locations of the thermal stimuli on the forearm. These results are shown in Fig. 5. As evident in Fig. 5 for both cold and warm stimuli, localization was more accurate for pulses delivered around the elbow as compared to the wrist ($F(1, 18) = 18.48, p < 0.001$). This may be due to the importance of anatomical landmarks such as the elbow or the spine in facilitating spatial localization as has been reported for the tactile modality [36].

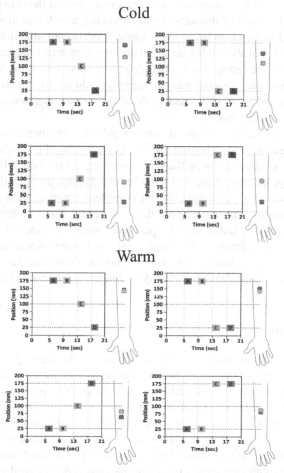

Fig. 5. Schematic depiction of the position of the physical stimuli on the graph and the group mean perceived position of those stimuli on the forearm. The dashed lines indicate the actual location of the Peltier modules on the arm.

A comparison of localization accuracy for cold and warmth reveals superior local-ization for the first cold stimulus as compared to the equivalent warm stimulus, although even for cold stimuli localization errors are still in the order of 10 mm. This result is consistent with those from other studies which have also reported better localization for cool than for warm stimuli [37]. These findings have been interpreted as indicating that the cold sensory system provides better somatotopic information than the warm sen-sory system. It is interesting to note, however, that the perceived location of the second stimulus delivered at the same location as the first changes much more when the skin is cooled as compared to warmed as shown by the greater spatial separation of the pulses in the upper plots in the figure as compared to the lower ones. The group mean change in perceived position between the first and second stimulus was 45 mm for cold stimuli as compared to 6 mm for warm stimuli. This difference may reflect the time course of the return to baseline skin temperature (i.e., the temperature of the skin prior to stimulus delivery) and/or the effect of the subsequent stimulus (pulse C) on thermal spatial processing, with cold localization being more labile. It is also possible that this divergence between warm and cold stimuli is due to the difference in their transience factors noted earlier (Fig. 2) with the sense of cold declining more rapidly than the sense of warmth. The design of the display ensured that participants could not use tactile cues to identify the location of the Peltier modules and so these localization differences reflect thermal and not tactile spatial processing.

The ability to localize a point of stimulation provides one metric that can be used to specify the configuration of a thermal display. For example, if users cannot distinguish between two sites of stimulation on the skin, then there is little added benefit associated with having a large number of thermal modules in a display, particularly if independent inputs are to be processed. A further caveat to consider in multi-element thermal displays is that for the thermal senses changing the area of stimulation affects the perceived intensity of the stimulus rather than its perceived spatial extent. What this means, is that a larger stimulus in terms of area is perceptually a more intense stimulus, a unique feature of the thermal modality. There is the potential, therefore, that when large areas of skin are heated or cooled the stimuli may no longer be innocuous but be perceived as painful.

4   Conclusions

As detailed in this paper, there are unique features of the thermal senses in terms of their temporal and spatial properties that need to be considered when designing thermo-tactile displays. In addition, due to differences between the senses of cold and warmth, various aspects of stimulus presentation such as the duration and time-varying profile of stimulation must be optimized for each sense. There is a considerable body of evidence indicating that sites beyond the hand are more effective at detecting and processing thermal cues. These locations should be considered for presenting thermal information and when coupled with tactile cues in a wearable device do not need to be co-located.

Acknowledgments. Research supported by the National Science Foundation under grant IIS-2006152, JSPS KAKENHI Grant Number 22H03679, and ULVAC-Hayashi MISTI Seed Fund, MIT-Japan Program.

References

1. Gallace, A., Spence, C.: In Touch with the Future. The Sense of Touch from Cognitive Neuroscience to Virtual Reality. Oxford University Press, New York (2014)
2. Dunkelberger, N., et al.: Improving perception accuracy with multi-sensory haptic cue delivery. In: Prattichizzo, D., Shinoda, H., Tan, H.Z., Ruffaldi, E., Frisoli, A. (eds.) EuroHaptics 2018. LNCS, vol. 10894, pp. 289–301. Springer, Cham (2018). https://doi.org/10.1007/978-3-319-93399-3_26

3. Jung, J., et al.: Speech communication through the skin: design of learning protocols and initial findings. In: Marcus, A., Wang, W. (eds.) DUXU 2018. LNCS, vol. 10919, pp. 447–460. Springer, Cham (2018). https://doi.org/10.1007/978-3-319-91803-7_34
4. Turcott, R., et al.: Efficient evaluation of coding strategies for transcutaneous language communication. In: Prattichizzo, D., Shinoda, H., Tan, H.Z., Ruffaldi, E., Frisoli, A. (eds.) Euro-Haptics 2018. LNCS, vol. 10894, pp. 600–611. Springer, Cham (2018). https://doi.org/10.1007/978-3-319-93399-3_51
5. Stein, B.E.: The New Handbook of Multisensory Processes. MIT Press, Cambridge (2012)
6. Ho, H.-N.: Material recognition based on thermal cues: mechanisms and applications. Temperature 5(1), 36–55 (2018). https://doi.org/10.1080/23328940.2017.1372042
7. Jones, L.A., Ho, H.-N.: Warm or cool, large or small? The challenge of thermal displays. IEEE Trans. Haptics 1, 53–70 (2008)
8. Drif, A., Citerin, J., Kheddar, A.: Thermal bilateral coupling in teleoperators. In: Proceedings of the 2005 IEEE/RSJ International Conference on Intelligent Robots and Systems (IROS), pp. 2818–2823. IEEE Press, New York (2005)
9. Ho, H.-N., Jones, L.A.: Development and evaluation of a thermal display for material identification and discrimination. ACM Trans. Appl. Percept. 4, 1–24 (2007)
10. Gabardi, M., Chiaradia, D., Leonardis, D., Solazzi, M., Frisoli, A.: A high performance thermal control for simulation of different materials in a fingertip haptic device. In: Prattichizzo, D., Shinoda, H., Tan, H.Z., Ruffaldi, E., Frisoli, A. (eds.) EuroHaptics 2018. LNCS, vol. 10894, pp. 313–325. Springer, Cham (2018). https://doi.org/10.1007/978-3-319-93399-3_28
11. Tewell, J., Bird, J., Buchanan, G.R.: The heat is on: a temperature display for conveying affective feedback. In: CHI 2017, pp. 1756–1767 (2017)
12. Tewell, J., Bird, J., Buchanan, G.R.: Heat-Nav: using temperature changes as navigational cues. In: CHI 2017, pp. 1131–1135 (2017)
13. Meng, X., Han, J., Chernyshov, G., Ragozin, K., Kunze, K.: ThermalDrive - towards situation awareness over thermal feedback in automated driving scenarios. In: Proceedings of the 27th International Conference on Intelligent User Interfaces, pp. 101–104 (2022)
14. Di Campli San Vito, P., Brewster, S., Pollick, F., Thompson, S., Skrypchuk, L., Mouzakitis, A.: Purring wheel: thermal and vibrotactile notifications on the steering wheel. In: Proceedings of the 19th ACM International Conference on Multimodal Interaction, pp. 461–469 (2020)
15. Singhal, A., Jones, L.A.: Dimensionality of thermal icons. In: IEEE World Haptics Conference, pp. 469–474. IEEE Press, New York (2015)
16. Halvey, M., Henderson, M., Brewster, S.A., Wilson, G., Hughes, S.A.: Augmenting media with thermal stimulation. In: Magnusson, C., Szymczak, D., Brewster, S. (eds.) HAID 2012. LNCS, vol. 7468, pp. 91–100. Springer, Heidelberg (2012). https://doi.org/10.1007/978-3-642-32796-4_10
17. Wettach, R., Danielsson, A., Behrens, C., Ness, T.: A thermal information display for mobile applications. In: Proceedings of the Mobile Human-Computer Interaction Conference 2007, pp. 182–185 (2007)
18. Wilson, G., Brewster, S., Halvey, M., Hughes, S.: Thermal feedback identification in a mobile environment. In: Oakley, I., Brewster, S. (eds.) HAID 2013. LNCS, vol. 7989, pp. 10–19. Springer, Heidelberg (2013). https://doi.org/10.1007/978-3-642-41068-0_2
19. Singhal, A., Jones, L.A.: Creating thermal icons – a model-based approach. ACM Trans. Appl. Percept. 15, 22 (2018). Article 14
20. Ho, H.-N., Sato, K., Kuroki, S., Watanabe, J., Maeno, T., Nishida, S.: Physical-perceptual correspondence for dynamic thermal stimulation. IEEE Trans. Haptics 10, 84–92 (2017)
21. Gallo, S., Rognini, G., Santos-Carreras, L., Vouga, T., Blanke, O., Bleuler, H.: Encoded and crossmodal thermal stimulation through a fingertip-sized haptic display. Front. Rob. AI 2 (2015). Article 25

22. Murakami, T., Fernando, C.L., Person, T., Minamizawa, K.: Altered touch: miniature haptic display with force, thermal and tactile feedback for augmented haptics. In: SIGGRAPH 2017 Emerging Technologies, pp. 1–2 (2017)
23. Leone, C., et al.: Conduction velocity of the cold spinal pathway in healthy humans. Eur. J. Pain **24**, 1923–1931 (2020). https://doi.org/10.1002/ejp.164
24. Yarnitsky, D., Ochoa, J.L.: Warm and cold specific somatosensory systems. Brain **114**, 1819–1826 (1991)
25. Singhal, A., Jones, L.A.: Perceptual interactions in thermo-tactile displays. In: IEEE World Haptics Conference, pp. 90–95. IEEE Press, New York (2017)
26. Stevens, J.C., Choo, K.C.: Temperature sensitivity of the body surface over the life span. Somatosens. Mot. Res. **15**, 13–28 (1998)
27. Filingeri, D.: Neurophysiology of skin thermal sensations. Compr. Physiol. **6**, 1429–1491 (2016)
28. Li., X., Petrini, L., Defrin, R., Madeleine, P., Arendt-Nielsen, L.: High resolution topographical mapping of warm and cold sensitivities. Clin. Neurophysiol. **119**, 2641–2646 (2008)
29. Johnson, K.O., Darian-Smith, I., LaMotte, C.: Peripheral neural determinants of temperature discrimination in man: a correlative study of responses to cooling skin. J. Neurophysiol. **36**, 347–370 (1973)
30. Filingeri, D., Zhang, H., Arens, E.A.: Thermosensory micromapping of warm and cold sensitivity across glabrous and hairy skin of male and female hands and feet. J. Appl. Physiol. **125**, 723–736 (2018)
31. Jones, L.A., Sarter, N.B.: Tactile displays: guidance for their design and application. Hum. Factors **50**, 90–111 (2008)
32. Vendrik, A.J.H., Eijkman, E.G.: Psychophysical properties determined with internal noise. In: Kenshalo, D.R. (ed.) The Skin Senses, pp. 178–193. Charles Thomas, Springfield (1968)
33. Nathan, P.W., Rice, R.C.: The localization of warm stimuli. Neurology **16**, 533–540 (1966)
34. Goldreich, D.: A Bayesian perceptual model replicates the cutaneous rabbit and other spatiotemporal illusions. PLoS ONE **2**, e333 (2007)
35. Singhal, A., Jones, L.: Space-time dependencies and thermal perception. In: Bello, F., Kajimoto, H., Visell, Y. (eds.) EuroHaptics 2016. LNCS, vol. 9774, pp. 291–302. Springer, Cham (2016). https://doi.org/10.1007/978-3-319-42321-0_27
36. Cholewiak, R.W., Brill, J.C., Schwab, A.: Vibrotactile localization on the abdomen: effects of place and space. Percept. Psychophys. **66**, 970–987 (2004)
37. Lee, D.K., McGillis, S.L.B., Greenspan, J.D.: Somatotopic localization of thermal stimuli: I. A comparison of within- versus across-dermatomal separation of innocuous thermal stimuli. Somatos. Mot. Res. **13**, 67–71 (1996)

The Relationship Between Frequency and Hand Region Actuated

Razvan Paisa(✉)[iD], Niels Christian Nilsson[iD], and Stefania Serafin[iD]

Multisensory Experience Lab, Aalborg University Copenhagen, Copenhagen, Denmark
rpa@create.aau.dk

Abstract. While the frequency response of the skin is described at macro level, there is a need to explore discrete areas of interest. The experiments described in this paper are part of a project that aims to build devices for cochlear implant (CI) users that meet music listening needs. The aim is to demonstrate that constant amplitude vibrotactile stimuli with distinct frequencies excite different areas of the hand with varying perceived intensity. 65 subjects took part in two within-subject experiments investigating the areas of the hand with most intense perceived sensation when exposed to various stimuli. Multinomial logistic regression was performed on the data and it was concluded that particular signals will elicit stronger sensations on some regions of the hand, and weaker on others. This indicates that there is a correlation between frequency of the stimuli and the area of the hand mostly stimulated.

Keywords: Tactile displays · Haptic devices · Tactile frequency response

1 Introduction

The skin is the largest organ of the human body, and besides its protective and temperature regulation functions, it affords the sense of touch - together with the somatosensory system. The psycho-perceptual properties of the skin, with respect to touch, have been studied extensively from multiple divergent angles. For the sake of conciseness, this article approaches the topic from the standpoint of musical augmentation for hearing impaired and cochlear implant (CI) users. Specifically, it demonstrates that distinct areas of the hand elicit a frequency dependent perception of vibrotactile stimuli, when stimulated from the same location. These findings allow tactile display designers to create novel devices with less technical complexity implied by multiple actuators.

2 Background and Related Work

Tactile stimuli are perceived through a series of complex mechanisms part of the somatosensory system; the fundamental agents are four types of mechanoreceptors: slowly adapting types 1 and 2, the Meissner corpuscle (colloquially known

© The Author(s), under exclusive license to Springer Nature Switzerland AG 2022
C. Saitis et al. (Eds.): HAID 2022, LNCS 13417, pp. 59–68, 2022.
https://doi.org/10.1007/978-3-031-15019-7_6

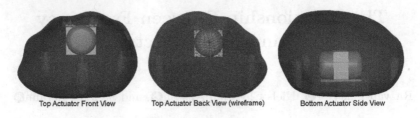

Top Actuator Front View   Top Actuator Back View (wireframe)   Bottom Actuator Side View

Fig. 1. See-through renders of the two versions of the VAM

as Rapid Adapting, RA) and the Pacinian corpuscle. These types of receptors respond differently to stimuli and elicit different sensations. In a musical context, the Meissner corspuscles and the Pacinian ones are known to be most useful [3,6,14]. The former ones have a high innervation density, and respond mostly to the range 1 Hz–100 Hz, with a peak sensitivity 40 Hz; the latter have a broader range 40 Hz to 1000 Hz, with maximum sensitivity around 250 Hz mark. Due to their larger size, Pacinian receptors have a lower spatial resolution compared to the Meissner corpuscles, and are known to respond mostly to vibrations [3,6,14]. While the parallel to the ear can be drawn, the frequency discrimination of the skin is far more complex and it is influenced by the amplitude, duration or the location of the stimuli, and not least by the multi-channel nature of the sensing system [1,10]. Because there is such a high variation, it would be incorrect to discuss of a single frequency response, therefore one should think of a range of responses, and focus on isolated body locus if possible [3,5]. In this paper we focus on the hand. The hand is one of the regions with the highest number of mechanoreceptors, specifically, the fingers are sensitive to a very wide frequency range from ~0.5 Hz to ~900 Hz [5,15]. However, these values are frequently challenged by new research, and there appears to be unknown confounding variables that affect these limits. A similar disagreement seems relevant to discussions about frequency discrimination thresholds, with researchers claiming that a difference of 4.6% would be enough to perceive different stimuli, while others suggest numbers closer to 30% [5,7,11]. When it comes to the spatial resolution measured by the classic cutaneous two-point discrimination test, the hand has thresholds between are 2 mm–8 mm, depending on the area [8]. Although sound and vibrotactile stimuli both are repeated changes in mechanical pressure captured by different receptors, it is hard to equate the two perception processes due to the radical differences in the sensing apparatus, as well as the lack of consensus in the literature. The mechanism linking auditory and tactile sensations is called multisensory integration, pioneered by [13]. It describes how humans form coherent, valid, and robust perception of reality, by processing sensory stimuli from various modalities. Multisensory integration suggests that enhancement can occur only for stimuli that are temporally coincident and propose that enhancement is strongest for those stimuli that individually are least effective. This mechanism seems to be playing a crucial role in the rehabilitation process of hearing loss and CI process, and it has been proven that deaf and CI users end up being better multisensory integrators than their hearing peers [12].

3   Materials

The tactile display used in this project is build around a Tactuator BM1C transducer, build by Tactile Labs, and was named VAM: *Vibrotactile Actuator for Music*. Other transducers like Haptuator Mk1 and Mk2 from the same manufacturer were tested in the setup, but their amplitude was too low. The Tactuator BM1C provides a much wider frequency response than can be perceived cutaneously, and the distortion (if any) is controlled due to the dampers encapsulating the actuator. These characteristics made it suitable for this project.

The tactile display was made exclusively for left hand usage, and had an ovoid shape as seen in Fig. 1 with the following dimensions: 84 mm wide, 58 mm tall and 89 mm deep. The shape was inspired by the resting hand position when fixed with an orthopedic splint. This pose should minimize the strain on the wrist while allowing the rest of the hand to relax, ensuring a similar holding pressure across the entire tactile display area. The enclosure was first modeled in clay ensuring that each digit has an ergonomic socket to rest into. The clay artefact was 3D scanned using Autodesk ReCap, by analyzing 40 still images of the subject, taken from multiple angles with a Fujifilm X-T1 camera and a Fujinon XF 35 mm @ f2.0 lens. Throughout this process, the clay prototype was suspended in mid air using transparent fishing line, in order to allow images to be captured from all angles. The resulting scan resulted in a high fidelity model but with chaotic topology, therefore a new 3D model was created, using the scan as an outline. This resulted in an accurate digital replica of the intended surface, ready for 3D printing. The model was split horizontally in two halves, that were hold together by three M3 × 16 bolts, and printed on an Ultimaker3 using PLA material. Two versions were constructed, one with the actuator resting on the bottom half, and the other with the actuator attached to the top half. This was done in order to be able to run experiments that account for the location of the actuator in respect to areas measured as shown in Fig. 2.

In order to ensure that the display had no resonant peaks that could influence the perception, its frequency response was measured on the interval 0–1000 kHz. The result was an average of 9 measured on 3 different locations, using a single axis from an ADXL355 analog accelerometer: tip of the middle finger socket,

Table 1. Filter parameters for compensation of resonant frequencies

Frequency (Hz)	15	30	60	100	150	200	250	300	500	800	1000
Bandwidth (Hz)	30	30	40	50	50	50	100	150	300	200	400
Gain (dB)		31	31	25	15	7	2	0	2	8	15	22

tip of thumb socket and lower palm. After measuring the frequency response, an approximate filter with inverse response was designed as a cascade of second order bandpass biquad filters with independent gains and bandwidths. The detailed filter parameters can be found in the Table 1 below.

Moreover, an attempt to account for the frequency response of the skin as reported by Merchel et al. was made with the same cascading biquad filters approach [9]. The goal was to ensure constant supra-threshold stimulation across the entire band of interest.

4   Evaluation

4.1   Goal

The experiments are part of a study on single-actuator, high-fidelity vibrotactile devices to be used by cochlear implant persons when listening to music. These experiments are at pre-paradigm stage, and they aim to explore the informal findings from previous observations and reports: the relationship between the frequency of the vibrotactile actuator and the area of hand where users perceived said vibrations. This goal translates into the following hypothesis: *people perceive distinct frequencies in different areas of the hand (thumb, fingers, palm, wrist, etc.), when stimulated by single-actuator vibrotactile handheld device with a constant supra-threshold amplitude.*

Moreover, the relation between frequencies and their areas of maximal perception was explored. The aim was to determine a potential mapping between vibrotactile frequency and excited hand area.

4.2   Experiments

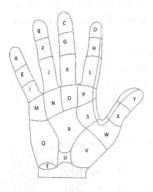

Fig. 2. Palm areas segmentation

Two within-subjects designed experiments were conducted with 35 (25M, 10F) and 32 (23M, 9F) participants respectively, that required them to indicate the areas of the hand where they felt the vibration the most. The only difference between the two experiments was the position of the actuator inside the VAM. Both designs can be seen in Fig. 1; experiment 1 was conducted with the actuator in the bottom half. The experiment had a multi-alternative (28) three forced choice design, that represents areas of the hand as seen in Fig. 2. The sinusoidal stimuli presented were first compensated according to the frequency response of the handheld device and then calibrated for constant supra threshold level (reference = 250 Hz) with a cascade of

2nd order biquad filters with F0 described in [9]. The 11 different stimuli presented had fixed frequencies ranging from 15 Hz to 1000 Hz, separated by a major third interval. Each stimuli lasted for 2 s, as there is evidence for no change in vibrotactile threshold of detection for stimuli longer that 1 s, although threshold could be higher for simulations shorter than 1 s [4,14].

4.3   Procedure

Participants were recruited among students and staff at Aalborg University Copenhagen. Participation was voluntary and no compensation was offered. The experiments lasted about 15 min and consisted of an accommodation phase followed by 3 simulations for each of the 11 frequencies. In the accommodation phase, the participants were instructed on the posture; they had to hold their hand on a soft, spongy surface throughout the experiment, to avoid the VAM touching the table, and potentially actuating it. Furthermore, they were exposed to an accommodation vibrotactile stimuli lasting one minute - a snipped of electronic music, in order to introduce the range of sensations possible, and allow the users to find a comfortable posture and relax the hand. When the music stimuli finished playing, the participant could proceed to the next phase.

Throughout the experimental phase, the participants were presented with one of the 11 stimuli, and were requested to rank the top 3 areas where they perceived the stimulation the most, by using the mouse to select the zones from the user interface (identical to Fig. 2). The participants had the opportunity to change the areas after initial selection, but they could not experience the stimuli again; this was done to ensure consistent exposure times between participants. Once the top 3 areas were selected, the users could continue to the next stimulation. The users had the possibility to select a "Not sensed" category, marked with "Ø" in Fig. 4. During the experiment, participants wore a pair of Bose QC700 noise canceling headphones playing pink noise at a comfortable level, with noise cancellation enabled on the highest setting. The data collected was anonymized, without the possibility of matching answers sets with participants. The following was logged: trial number (1–33), stimuli frequency, 1st, 2nd, 3rd selected area, and the log file creation time.

5   Results

The data from the two experiments was treated as categorical, and analyzed separately. First, the distribution of preferences was analysed, and then the data was inserted into a predictive model to compare tendencies and determine if the frequency of the stimuli (as the independent variable) can explain the differences in those trends.

Descriptive Statistics: Fig. 3 shows the sum of preferences for each frequency. We present the sum instead of the top 3 individual rankings for two reasons: (1) For experiment 1, the highest ranking areas across the conditions was always option "Y" - the closest to the physical location to the actuator. This is assumed to be a bias towards that location, but a further test is planned to confirm it. (2) During post-experiment interviews, participants reported not ranking the sensations based on perceived intensity, but instead the presence of sensation in the selected locations. These two factors pointed towards a low validity of reported ranks, thus each answer was treated with equal importance. Initial results show that the perception of all frequencies seem to peak towards finger tips, as well as the palmar digital area, and be almost not existent closest to the wrist (areas, "T", "U", "Q"); a fact that can be explained by the shape, size and grip of the VAM. Besides that, it's noticeable that different frequencies excited distinct areas of the hand, especially 171 Hz, 256 Hz 384 Hz for experiment 1 51 Hz, 76 Hz, 577 Hz for experiment 2. These areas are felt around the proximal phalanges while other frequencies are perceived on areas closest to the actuator's position (X-Y for experiment 1, and N-O for experiment 2). The three frequencies from experiment 1 are closest to the peak response of the Pacinian Corpuscles [2], indicating that even though there could be an amplitude based bias (due to the physical proximity to the actuator), some frequencies elicit vibrotactile sensations in different areas of the hand. However, this cannot be concluded based on a frequency-location relation alone.

Multinomial regression model with mixed effects: To understand if there is a difference between the areas, a multinomial regression model was created that predicts the probability of selecting any of the areas by the explanatory variable: the frequency, that was treated as numerical and continuous. This is a matter of trying to parameterize the probability of selecting any of the areas in terms of baseline probability and the effect of the frequency. However, first it is important to account for the repeated measurement, by introducing a user-based random effect, and only after account for the fixed effect (frequency).

In order to run the multinomial regression model without over-parameterizing it, a reference area was selected, and the probability of choosing another area than the the reference was computed, for each frequency. In the case of experiment 1, the reference area was "Y", while for the experiment 2 it was "O"; this was done to challenge the bias introduced by the difference in amplitude as a result of distance-based energy dissipation within the VAM. In order to reach convergence of the model, some areas with too limited samples were aggregated into a zone; for experiment 1 areas "T", "U", "Q" were combined to create area "TUQ", and for experiment 2, area "T" and "U" were aggregated into zone "TU", as seen in Fig. 4.

After the prediction model was created, another identical model was created without accounting for frequency. The two models were compared with a *F test* that clarifies whether adding the frequency term is a significant contribution to the prediction model. In the case of both experiments there was a significant difference between the model accounting for frequency and the one that did not, with significance level (p-value) smaller than machine precision (e^{-16} and e^{-14} respectively). This results confirms the hypothesis stated in 4 and the variability

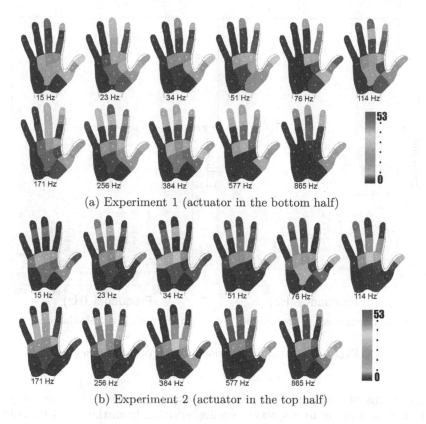

(a) Experiment 1 (actuator in the bottom half)

(b) Experiment 2 (actuator in the top half)

Fig. 3. Distribution of summed preferred areas

observed in the choice of area can be explained by frequency, as predicted by the models described above.

6 Discussion

The results related to located perception of stimuli with different frequencies suggest that there is a significant difference between the stimuli frequencies, in terms of area where they are perceived the most. Nevertheless, there is not enough data relative to the complexity of the model to allow for accurate pairwise analysis (e.g., the chance of selecting middle finger tip compared to the index finger tip, for any given frequency), but the data represented in Fig. 4 clearly show that areas closer to the actuator for both experiments ("X", "Y", "W" and "N", "O", "P") have a much greater chance for lower frequencies, than higher ones. Conversely, some areas closer to fingertips have higher chances for being selected as the frequency increases; this behavior is in line with previous studies investigatin the amplitude sensing properties of the skin [5,15]. As a result, there is evidence that the fingertips have the broadest sensing capacity of the body, not

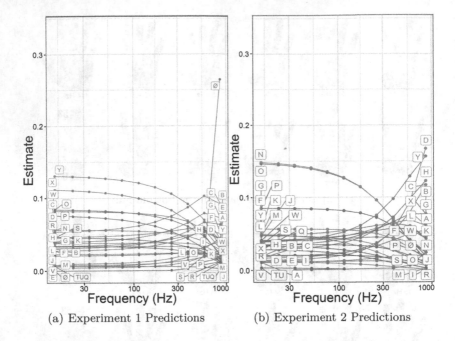

(a) Experiment 1 Predictions   (b) Experiment 2 Predictions

Fig. 4. Predicted distribution of areas over frequency

only in terms of amplitude, but also frequency. Moreover, the results suggests that there is a decay in frequency sensing, starting from the tip of the middle finger and decreasing radially.

While both experiments suggest that there are ares that sense differently, the results hint that these differences depend highly on the design of tactile display. The position of the actuator, and probably more important, the contact point for it, influences the distribution of perceived frequencies. Throughout this study the position and the contact point were correlated, therefore it's impossible to identify which of the two explains the variation of the data between experiment one and two. One interesting observation is that the "Not sensed (Ø)" category is more prominent in the first experiment than the second one, especially at the highest frequencies tested, indicating that there is a somewhat higher sensitivity to the upper spectrum when the actuator is closer to the metacarpal area.

To our knowledge, this study is among the first that evaluate the characteristics of the skin on multiple points, with a single actuator, as opposite to the traditional approach of evaluating the sole point of contact. Of course, there is a potential limitation in measuring the frequency response accurately with a single actuator, therefore there's a need to challenge the findings from this article with a different setup that could offer greater control over the stimuli delivered at each area of the hand. Nevertheless, given the nature of the larger project this study belongs to, it is valuable to explore haptic perception in relation to a device designed explicitly for CI users' music listening. This is important to underline as there is a need for further rigorous investigation through the same paradigm, in order to fully understand the vibrotactile properties of the skin.

7 Conclusions

This study proposes a single-actuator handheld tactile display that allows users to sense stimuli across the entire spectrum of the skin. Two separate devices were constructed with different actuator placements. The displays used in two users studies that evaluated the perception of vibrotactile stimuli with various frequencies, over 27 discrete areas. The results indicate that there is a difference in perception area that is dependent of the frequency of the stimuli. While the data is insufficient for accurate comparison of each frequency-area combination, at least by using multinomial regression, the probability of selecting areas closest to the actuator is higher at lower frequencies and the finger tips show highest sensitivity as the frequency increases. For years, there has been an interest in the vibrotactile properties of the human skin. This research contributes to this debate, by showing, not only that distinct areas of the hand sense frequency with variate intensity, but also that it's possible to create a single actuator tactile display that will stimulate the human hand in multiple areas.

Acknowledgments. This work is supported by NordForsk's Nordic University Hub and Nordic Sound and Music Computing Network (NordicSMC).

References

1. Birnbaum, D.M., Wanderley, M.M.: A systematic approach to musical vibrotactile feedback (2007)
2. Brisben, A.J., Hsiao, S.S., Johnson, K.O.: Detection of vibration transmitted through an object grasped in the hand. J. Neurophysiol. **81**(4), 1548–1558 (1999). https://doi.org/10.1152/jn.1999.81.4.1548
3. Chafe, C.: Tactile audio feedback (1993)
4. Hopkins, C., Maté-Cid, S., Fulford, R., Seiffert, G., Ginsborg, J.: Vibrotactile presentation of musical notes to the glabrous skin for adults with normal hearing or a hearing impairment: thresholds, dynamic range and high-frequency perception. PLoS ONE **11**(5), e0155807 (2016). https://doi.org/10.1371/journal.pone.0155807
5. Jones, L.A., Sarter, N.B.: Tactile displays: guidance for their design and application. Hum. Factors **50**(1), 90–111 (2008). https://doi.org/10.1518/001872008X250638
6. Kyung, K.U., Ahn, M., Kwon, D.S., Srinivasan, M.A.: Perceptual and biomechanical frequency response of human skin: implication for design of tactile displays (2005). https://doi.org/10.1109/WHC.2005.105
7. Mahns, D.A., Perkins, N.M., Sahai, V., Robinson, L., Rowe, M.J.: Vibrotactile frequency discrimination in human hairy skin. J. Neurophysiol. **95**(3), 1442–1450 (2006). https://doi.org/10.1152/jn.00483.2005
8. Mancini, F., et al.: Whole-body mapping of spatial acuity for pain and touch. Ann. Neurol. **75**(6), 917–924 (2014). https://doi.org/10.1002/ana.24179

9. Merchel, S., Altinsoy, M.E.: Psychophysical comparison of the auditory and tactile perception: a survey. J. Multimodal User Interfaces **14**(3), 271–283 (2020). https://doi.org/10.1007/s12193-020-00333-z
10. Morley, J.W., Rowe, M.J.: Perceived pitch of vibrotactile stimuli: effects of vibration amplitude, and implications for vibration frequency coding. J. Physiol. **431**(1), 403–416 (1990). https://doi.org/10.1113/jphysiol.1990.sp018336
11. Mowbray, G.H., Gebhard, J.W.: Sensitivity of the skin to changes in rate of intermittent mechanical stimuli. Science **125**(3261), 1297–1298 (1957). https://doi.org/10.1126/science.125.3261.1297
12. Rouger, J., Lagleyre, S., Fraysse, B., Deneve, S., Deguine, O., Barone, P.: Evidence that cochlear-implanted deaf patients are better multisensory integrators. Proc. Natl. Acad. Sci. U.S.A. **104**(17), 7295–7300 (2007). https://doi.org/10.1073/pnas.0609419104
13. Stein, B., Stein, P., Meredith, M.: The Merging of the Senses. A Bradford Book, MIT Press (1993). https://books.google.se/books?id=uCV9QgAACAAJ
14. Verrillo, R.T.: Vibration sensation in humans. Music. Percept. **9**(3), 281–302 (1992). https://doi.org/10.2307/40285553
15. Wilska, A.: On the vibrational sensitivity in different regions of the body surface. Acta Physiol. Scand. **31**(2–3), 285–289 (1954). https://doi.org/10.1111/j.1748-1716.1954.tb01139.x

Perceptual Evaluation of the Quantization Level of a Vibrotactile Signal

Quentin Consigny[1]($\boxtimes$)(iD), Arthur Paté[2](iD), and Jean-Loïc Le Carrou[1](iD)

[1] Sorbonne Université, CNRS, Institut d'Alembert UMR 7190, LAM, Paris, France
quentin.consigny@etu.sorbonne-universite.fr,
jean-loic.le_carrou@sorbonne-universite.fr
[2] Univ. Lille, CNRS, Centrale Lille, Univ. Polytechnique Hauts-de-France, Junia,
UMR 8520 - IEMN, 59000 Lille, France
arthur.pate@junia.com

Abstract. The quantization of vibrotactile signals is generally performed in the same way as for audio signals. However, the specificities of the sense of touch may allow other choices for the digitization of vibrotactile signals, in particular on the number of quantization bits. The objective of this paper is to define the minimal number of quantization bits, ensuring an imperceptible digitization to touch. For this, a perceptual study is conducted on a set of signals for several quantization levels. For each signal, the total perceptible harmonic distortion (PTHD), taking into account the vibrotactile thresholds, is defined and calculated. PTHD seems to predict a threshold from which the quantization level of the vibrotactile signals is perceptible. This result was obtained by a perceptive study carried out on 29 subjects from pairwise comparison with vibrotactile signals emitted by an electrodynamic transducer placed in a wristband. If the PTHD of a vibrotactile signal is less than 35 dB, the digitization effect will be imperceptible. This suggests that 8-bit DACs may be sufficient to generate vibrotactile signals without the digitization effects being perceptible.

Keywords: Vibrotactile · Quantization · Perception · Psychophysics

1 Introduction

When digitizing audio signals, the number of quantization bits used is an important parameter to consider. Digitizing a signal introduces harmonic distortions. Because they are signals with a frequency content in the 10–1000 Hz band, vibrotactile signals are often designed by computers as audio signals. This makes it possible to take advantage of existing tools for sound design when designing vibrotactile signals. However, our perception of the digitization (of the same signal) can change if this signal is heard or perceived by touch.

According to the literature, the skin is sensitive to vibrotactile signals between 5 Hz [3] and 1 kHz [21]. Sensitivity is highest around 250 Hz [11,21,22].

The iso-sensitivity curves (U-shaped) show that our sensitivity decreases rapidly above 250 Hz. The envelop of the signal has been shown to play a much more significant role than its spectrum in how we perceive vibrotactile signals [5,23]. Regarding the perception of the frequencies, to the best of our knowledge, the vibrotactile frequency discrimination threshold (JND) is systematically greater than 10% and regularly exceeds 25% [15]. However, it is possible to discriminate voices of different speakers, but also instruments (playing the same note) by perceiving their sound only in vibrotactile form. Concerning the quantization level of signals, some studies suggest that 8-bit DACs are sufficient to be used for the generation of vibrotactile signals [9,13,14], which may seem low with respect to audio standards. However, there is no perceptual study of the quantization level for vibrotactile signals. So it should be formally demonstrated, this motivates the present study.

For all the studies found so far, the signals are applied to the fingers [1,5,15,21], arms [13], back [13], thighs [16], skull [12] or perioral area [3]. There is a lack of information about the wrist. However, this area is sensitive to vibrotactile signals [10], limits bone conduction, and can be used without disturbing instrumental practice (for most instruments and tools, e.g. musical instruments) or any other manipulation involving the use of hands. In addition, wearing a miniature exciter on the wrist is unlikely to disturb people already used to wear a watch [18].

In summary, the current scientific literature does not allow us to predict to what extent the quantization effects are perceptible when the vibrotactile signals are played on the wrist.

This paper presents a perceptual study of vibrotactile signal quantization to determine what level of quantization can be perceptible on the skin of the human wrist. After a detailed presentation of the method and material used for this study in Sect. 2, the results are given in Sect. 3. The descriptors (total harmonic distortion and perceptual total harmonic distortion) are used to interpret the discrimination threshold of the vibrotactile signal quantization level in Sect. 4.

This information about the threshold of perception of digitization may influence the choice of the digital-to-analog converter (DAC). The aim of the present study is to determine which level of quantization of the signal is perceptible to our sense of touch for basic signals.

2   Method

On the electronics market, there are many 2, 4, 8 and 16 bit DACs[1]. Therefore, the choice is made to test vibrotactile signals quantized on these 4 levels. For an n-bit quantization, a series of allowed values is created by distributing the values between -1 and 1 in an equidistant way. For each sampling, the value of the digital signal corresponds to the closest allowed value of the analog signal. This allows to have a rigorously constant signal dynamic for all quantization levels.

---

[1] www.mouser.com/c/semiconductors/data-converter-ics/.

Thus, a normalized analog sine will be transformed, after a quantization on a single bit into a succession of −1 and 1. Whereas for a quantization on 2 bits, the signal would be transformed into a succession of −1, −0.33, 0.33 and 1.

For that, a pairwise comparison is made between vibrotactile signals. Only the quantization level changes between them (identical frequency, amplitude, etc.). The objective is to know if these signals are perceived as identical or not.

During preliminary tests, it was observed that we could not distinguish between a 16-bit coded vibrotactile signal and an analog signal (created with a low-frequency signal generator). The 16-bit signals will be therefore considered as "pseudo-analog" (they are not analog signals but can be considered as such in terms of perception). Regarding the sampling rate, a frequency of 44,100 Hz (twice the upper limit of audio frequency perception) is used. Vibrotactile signals may certainly be quantized at 2 kHz considering that the human sensitivity does not exceed 1 kHz [21]).

The hypothesis is that, compared to digital audio signals, the number of bits used to quantize a vibrotactile signal without introducing a touch-perceptible quantization effect can be reduced. This is what the literature suggests (see Sect. 1). Preliminary studies seem to show that it would be possible to use 8-bit digital-to-analog converters (DAC) without distinguishing their output signal from an analog output.

2.1 Experimental Protocol

Four quantization levels are considered for the vibrotactile signals: 2, 4, 8, and 16 quantization bits. The quantized signals are:

- A sine wave near the frequency at which the skin is the most sensitive to the vibrotactile signals (225 Hz) [20,21].
- A sine wave (45 Hz) close to the lower limit of vibrotactile sensitivity, whose quantization effects (mainly the introduction of harmonics [6,17]) appear at 225 Hz (the 5th harmonic, and also the frequency of maximal sensitivity).
- A sine wave with a frequency in between these last two frequencies: 135 Hz. The skin has an intermediate sensitivity (compared to 45 and 225 Hz) to this frequency. The amount of harmonics generated is also intermediate.

Participants have to compare two signals (A and B). The participants can experience the signals as many times as they wish, and in any order they like. The signals have a duration of 1.5 s. In order to prevent any response based on intensity, the energy is normalized between the signals. To avoid being influenced by the sound that may be radiated by the actuator, the participants wore earplugs and headphones in which white noise is played.

The signals of each presented pair have the same frequency and the same amplitude. The only variable is the number of bits used for quantization. Each pair is presented twice. For four levels of quantization and two frequencies, this represents sixty pairs to compare (2 times × 3 frequencies × (4 + 3 + 2 + 1) pairs). These sixty pairs are all mixed. The order of presentation is pseudorandom and balanced across participants (a balanced Latin square is used).

The instruction given to the participant is: "You can play the signals in any order you like. You can play each signal as many times as you want. Indicate, for each pair of signals, if you perceive these signals as different or identical".

2.2 Material

It is verified that the sound card (a Focusrite Scarlett 2i2)[2] does not introduce any additional quantization effect. In order to play the vibrotactile signals (A and B) via the wristband and to be able to indicate whether these signals are perceived as the same or different, the participant is presented with a Launchpad Novation XL interface[3] (see Fig. 1). Vibrotactile signals are generated with a DAEX13CT-8 (by Dayton Audio) transducer[4]. To adapt the signal of the sound card to this equipment, the signal of the Scarlett 2i2 is amplified with an amplifier FX1002A[5] which delivers a signal with a nominal voltage of 3.3 V. The transducer is placed on the inside of the wrist of the non-dominant hand.

According to the literature [20], the threshold of perception depends on the vibrating surface. An increase of this surface allows to perceive weaker signals. From a certain threshold value (e.g. 3 cm on the finger [20]), increasing the vibrating surface no longer increases (but does not decrease [20]) the sensitivity of the skin. That is why a 1.5-cm radius plexiglas disc is fixed at the end of the actuator. This disc is in contact with the skin (see Fig. 2). This disc gives a vibrating surface maximizing the sensitivity of the skin to the vibrotactile signals.

A preliminary test is used to determine an output intensity that allows the signals to be easily felt without being heard. During the test, this intensity is used for all participants. Then the displacement of the actuator is measured with a μEpsilon ILD1750-10[6]. On the entire vibrotactile spectrum, this displacement is between 0.8 mm and 3 mm. Then using Verrillo's iso-sensitivity curves for this displacement [21], a filter is created to have a perceptually equal intensity for the 3 quantized sines. The equation of this curve has been graphically approximated and is given in Eq. 1 where G is the gain (in dB) obtained for a frequency f (in Hertz).

$$G(f) = -36.5 + 0.417f - 1.62 \times 10^{-3}f^2 + 2.47 \times 10^{-6}f^3 - 1.33 \times 10^{-9}f^4 \quad (1)$$

3   Results

For this study, 29 participants made a series of comparisons. Each pair is presented twice; the experiment is conducted for 3 different levels of tightening

---

[2] www.focusrite.com/en/usb-audio-interface/scarlett/scarlett-2i2.
[3] www.novationmusic.com/en/launch/launchpad-x.
[4] www.daytonaudio.com/product/1173.
[5] www.audiophonics.fr/en/search?search_query=FX-AUDIO+FX1002A+.
[6] www.micro-epsilon.com/download/manuals/man–optoNCDT-1750–en.pdf.

Fig. 1. The interface used by the participants

Fig. 2. A vibrotactile wristband

of the wristband: loose, normal and strong. The wristband used notches. The participant is asked to fix the wristband with a comfortable tightening; this tightening defines the normal position. Then the strong tightening is obtained by increasing the tightening by two notches (this is equivalent to reducing the circumference of the wristband by 5 mm). The weak tightening, on the contrary, is obtained by decreasing the tightening by two notches. The results of the three tightening are merged for this analysis.

To present the results obtained, a similarity index S is defined. This index, for each participant and for each pair of signals, corresponds to the number of responses "signals perceived as identical" divided by the total number of presentations for each pair: $S = \frac{N_{same}}{N_{presentation}}$. For each tightening (strong, normal and light), each pair is presented twice. A participant provides a total of 6 responses for each pair. N_{same} is therefore an integer between 0 and 6 and $N_{presentation}$ is always 6. For each of these sets of 6 responses, the mean similarity index between participants (and standard deviation) are calculated and shown in Table 1.

4 Analysis

4.1 Spectral Effect Analysis

A decrease in the number of bits used to quantize the signal introduces a greater quantization error. This quantization error is mainly reflected by adding harmonics in the spectrum [2,4]. This phenomenon of introducing harmonics from the analog signal into the digital signal is called "harmonic distortion". This distortion has already been formulated for vibrotactile signals [7]. To predict this harmonic distortion, the "total harmonic distortion" (THD) can be calculated. The THD is defined as the ratio of the square of the sum of the amplitudes of all harmonic components (except the fundamental frequency) to the amplitude

Table 1. Mean similarity index, standard deviation, and difference of perceptual total harmonic distortion (Δ PTHD), with a definition given in part Sect. 4.1 obtained during the comparisons of each pair.

	Compared quantization (in bits)	2 vs 2	2 vs 4	2 vs 8	2 vs 16	4 vs 4	4 vs 8	4 vs 16	8 vs 8	8 vs 16	16 vs 16
45 Hz	*Similarity index*	**0.71**	**0.12**	**0.11**	**0.11**	**0.74**	**0.86**	**0.72**	**0.73**	**0.79**	**0.79**
	Standard deviation	*0.17*	*0.11*	*0.12*	*0.11*	*0.18*	*0.15*	*0.18*	*0.18*	*0.17*	*0.15*
	Δ PTHD (in dB)	0	36	38	45	0	27	33	0	7	0
135 Hz	*Similarity index*	**0.68**	**0.63**	**0.67**	**0.68**	**0.68**	**0.70**	**0.85**	**0.77**	**0.70**	**0.76**
	Standard deviation	*0.16*	*0.19*	*0.19*	*0.16*	*0.16*	*0.19*	*0.18*	*0.16*	*0.19*	*0.16*
	Δ PTHD (in dB)	0	32	33	32	0	21	29	0	8	0
225 Hz	*Similarity index*	**0.87**	**0.87**	**0.83**	**0.83**	**0.89**	**0.80**	**0.98**	**0.93**	**0.75**	**0.75**
	Standard deviation	*0.15*	*0.16*	*0.17*	*0.16*	*0.15*	*0.15*	*0.17*	*0.17*	*0.16*	*0.15*
	Δ PTHD (in dB)	0	5	23	32	0	18	27	0	9	0

of the fundamental frequency [6, 17]. With v_i the amplitude of the ith harmonic, where 1 corresponds to the fundamental frequency, the THD is obtained as in Eq. 2 :

$$THD = \frac{\sqrt{\sum_{i=2}^{\infty} v_i^2}}{v_1} \qquad (2)$$

As defined, the THD treats each frequency equally. However, human sensitivity to the vibrotactile signal varies according to the considered frequency (see Verrillo's U-shaped iso-sensitivity curves [21]). If the THD allows to predict the quantity of harmonics produced by the quantization, the calculation of a "perceptual" THD may be introduced. In order to obtain this perceptual total harmonic distortion (PTHD), a coefficient (called C_i for the ith harmonic) is applied on each element of the digital spectrum according to the inverse iso-sensitivity curves from Verrillo. The PTHD defined is in Eq. 3 :

$$PTHD = \frac{\sqrt{\sum_{i=2}^{\infty} C_i v_i^2}}{v_1} \qquad (3)$$

The assumption made here is that the spectrum corrected by the gains defined in Eq. 1 approximates well the spectrum of the perceived signal. Then, a THD is computed from the modified spectrum. The method to obtain THD and PTHD is illustrated in Fig. 3.

During the comparison of two signals, the difference between the PTHDs of each signal can be studied. If the PTHD is indeed related to the perceptible level of harmonic distortion (and thus to the quantization level used), the PTHD difference (named ΔPTHD with: $\Delta\text{PTHD}_{i,j} = |PTHD_i - PTHD_j|$ where PTHD_n is the PTHD of a signal quantized with n bits) of each pair should be correlated to the similarity index of that pair. The ΔPTHD of each pair is given in Table 1.

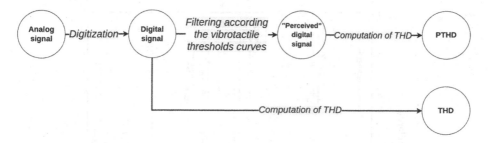

Fig. 3. Total harmonic distortion (THD) and perceptual total harmonic distortion (PTHD) calculations.

4.2 Analysis of the Results of the Perceptual Test

For each pair of signals and each participant, the similarity index S is computed. The mean and standard deviation of each index are given in Table 1. It also provides the PTHD deviation (ΔPTHD) of each pair.

Each of these pairs is shown in Fig. 4 by a point. The horizontal axis of this figure represents the ΔPTHD of the pair and the vertical axis represents the similarity index of this pair. It seems that below a certain value of Δ PTHD (around 35 dB) the similarity index is constant (around 0.8). Then it suddenly decreases to an asymptotic value of about 0.2. These points seem to be distributed according to a sigmoid whose equation is estimated from a least squares method (see Fig. 4).

This kind of curve is the classical psychophysical threshold [19]. This suggests that there is a threshold of ΔPTHD (about 35 dB with the test of this study and with a vibrotactile signal played on the inside of the wrist) below which the effects of quantization would not be perceptible.

For identical signals, the similarity index should be very close to 1. However, in Table 1, this value is more often around 0.8. It means that when 2 identical signals are presented, the participant's response is "identical" in approximately 80% of cases. One hypothesis that could explain this value is that participants tried to balance their responses, i.e. gave overall the same number of "identical" and "different" responses. They also felt a sense of failure by not being able to perceive a difference, as described by some participants.

5   Discussion

The PTHD definition appears to be effective. It predicts the similarity index of the compared pairs correctly ($R^2 = 0.93$).

For a PTHD lower than 35 dB, the similarity index of the compared signals is stable (approximately 0.8). A few dB above these 35 dB, the similarity index tends rapidly towards a new asymptot (0.2). This suggests that the quantization effects of the vibrotactile signals are undetectable above a threshold value of PTHD of 35 dB.

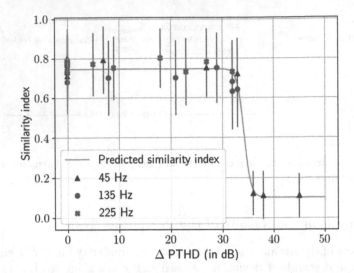

Fig. 4. Actual (points represented by different markers according to fundamental frequency) and predicted (orange line representing by equation $S = 0.75 + \frac{0.65}{1+e^{1.5 \times \Delta PTHD}}$) similarity index according to the difference in THD between the two elements of the pair. The points represent the mean similarity indexes and the vertical bars represent the standard deviation of the set. (Color figure online)

The PTHD value, unlike the THD, does not depend only on the number of bits used to quantize the signal. It also takes into account the spectrum of the quantized signal. Devices using only the 250–400 Hz frequency band and simple signals (sine) have already been designed [11,22]. In this band, the PTHD decreases rapidly (more than 10 dB) with the addition of an extra quantization bit. Thus in this frequency range, the use of 2-bit DACs could be considered.

For more common applications, the DACs that are regularly found on embedded boards (Arduino, Raspberry, etc.), which are 8-bit DACs, could be used without degrading the quality of the vibrotactile signals over the entire vibrotactile spectrum. The use of this kind of DAC is less expensive and simpler to set up, but it also offers other advantages. By sending data from a network to a DAC on 8 instead of 24 bits the quantity of data to be sent is divided by three.

Redefining this perceptual limit of quantization level helps to better understand our perception of vibrotactile signals. The observations from this study could facilitate future designs of vibrotactile signals. Variations (of spectrum, envelop, etc.) contained in the vibrotactile signal that cannot be represented when encoded with 8 bits will presumably not be perceptible to the sense of touch.

6   Conclusion

The objective of this article was first to confirm that the quantization of vibrotactile signals on 8 bits could be imperceptible, and then to propose a threshold of perception of the level of quantization of vibrotactile signals. For that, a comparison by pair of vibrotactile signals quantized on different numbers of bits has been carried out. In addition, an analysis of the total harmonic distortion (THD) was made for these signals, and then a definition of perceptible total harmonic distortion (PTHD) was proposed. The obtained results seem to confirm that a quantization of the vibrotactile signals on 8 bits is not perceptible. It would seem that significant differences in PTHD (at least 30 dB) must be present to make perceptible the harmonic distortion due to quantization.

The work presented here could be continued and improved in different ways. A specific study of the threshold of perception of ΔPTHD would be interesting and would refine our observations. The filters used did not take into account the behavior of the transducer. A protocol allowing the characterization of the actuator coupled to the skin would allow to obtain measurements closer to the present experimental conditions [8]. This perceptual study has been conducted with extremely simple signals (3 sines of 2 s with a constant envelop). A work focusing on more complex signals is now required.

Acknowledgements. This work is funded by a grant from the French National Research Agency (ANR) as part of the "Staccato" Project (ANR–19–CE38–0008–01).

References

1. Ammirante, P., Russo, F.A., Good, A., Fels, D.I.: Feeling voices. PLoS ONE **8**(1), e53585 (2013). https://doi.org/10.1371/journal.pone.0053585
2. Balestrieri, E., Rapuano, S.: Defining DAC performance in the frequency domain. Measurement **40**(5), 463–472 (2007). https://doi.org/10.1016/j.measurement.2006.12.004
3. Barlow, S.: Adaptive vibrotactile threshold estimation of the glabrous hand and perioral face following MCA stroke. Biomed. J. Sci. Tech. Res. **23** (2019). https://doi.org/10.26717/BJSTR.2019.23.003899
4. Bennett, W.R.: Spectra of quantized signals. Bell Syst. Tech. J. **27**(3), 446–472 (1948). https://doi.org/10.1002/j.1538-7305.1948.tb01340.x
5. Birnbaum, D., Wanderley, M.: A systematic approach to musical vibrotactile feedback. In: International Computer Music Conference, ICMC 2007 (2011)
6. Blagouchine, I.V., Moreau, E.: Analytic method for the computation of the total harmonic distortion by the Cauchy method of residues. IEEE Trans. Commun. **59**(9), 2478–2491 (2011). https://doi.org/10.1109/tcomm.2011.061511.100749
7. Bukkapatnam, A.T., Depalle, P., Wanderley, M.M.: Defining a vibrotactile toolkit for digital musical instruments: characterizing voice coil actuators, effects of loading, and equalization of the frequency response. J. Multimodal User Interfaces **14**(3), 285–301 (2020). https://doi.org/10.1007/s12193-020-00340-0
8. Consigny, Q., Paté, A., Le Carrou, J.L., Genevois, H.: Caractérisation par l'étude de l'impédance électrique d'un transducteur électro-dynamique mécaniquement chargé par différents matériaux. In: Proceedings of the Congrès Français d'Acoustique, Marseille, France (2022). (in French)
9. Frisson, C., Decaudin, J., Sanz Lopez, M., Pietrzak, T.: Printgets: an open-source toolbox for designing vibrotactile widgets with industrial-grade printed actuators and sensors. In: International Workshop on Haptic and Audio Interaction Design, Montreal, Canada (2020)

10. Islam, M.S., Lim, S.: Vibrotactile feedback in virtual motor learning: a systematic review. Appl. Ergon. **101**, 103694 (2022). https://doi.org/10.1016/j.apergo.2022.103694
11. Jones, L.A., Sarter, N.B.: Tactile displays: guidance for their design and application. Hum. Fact. J. Hum. Fact. Ergon. Soc. **50**(1), 90–111 (2008). https://doi.org/10.1518/001872008x250638
12. Kim, M., Abdulali, A., Jeon, S.: Rendering vibrotactile flow on backside of the head: initial study. In: 2018 IEEE Games, Entertainment, Media Conference (GEM). IEEE (2018). https://doi.org/10.1109/gem.2018.8516545
13. Mirzaei, M., Kán, P., Kaufmann, H.: Effects of using vibrotactile feedback on sound localization by deaf and hard-of-hearing people in virtual environments. Electronics **10**(22), 2794 (2021). https://doi.org/10.3390/electronics10222794
14. Pantera, L., Hudin, C.: Multitouch vibrotactile feedback on a tactile screen by the inverse filter technique: vibration amplitude and spatial resolution. IEEE Trans. Haptics **13**(3), 493–503 (2020). https://doi.org/10.1109/toh.2020.2981307
15. Pongrac, H.: Vibrotactile perception: examining the coding of vibrations and the just noticeable difference under various conditions. Multimedia Syst. **13**(4), 297–307 (2007). https://doi.org/10.1007/s00530-007-0105-x
16. Salzer, Y., Oron-Gilad, T., Ronen, A., Parmet, Y.: Vibrotactile "on-thigh" alerting system in the cockpit. Hum. Fact. J. Hum. Fact. Ergon. Soc. **53**(2), 118–131 (2011). https://doi.org/10.1177/0018720811403139
17. Shmilovitz, D.: On the definition of total harmonic distortion and its effect on measurement interpretation. IEEE Trans. Power Deliv. **20**(1), 526–528 (2005). https://doi.org/10.1109/tpwrd.2004.839744
18. Terenti, M., Vatavu, R.D.: Measuring the user experience of vibrotactile feedback on the finger, wrist, and forearm for touch input on large displays. In: CHI Conference on Human Factors in Computing Systems Extended Abstracts. ACM (2022). https://doi.org/10.1145/3491101.3519704
19. Treutwein, B., Strasburger, H.: Fitting the psychometric function. Percept. Psychophys. **61**(1), 87–106 (1999). https://doi.org/10.3758/bf03211951
20. Verrillo, R.T.: Psychophysics of vibrotactile stimulation. J. Acoust. Soc. Am. **77**(1), 225–232 (1985). https://doi.org/10.1121/1.392263
21. Verrillo, R.T.: Vibration sensation in humans. Music. Percept. **9**(3), 281–302 (1992). https://doi.org/10.2307/40285553
22. Wilska, A.: On the vibrational sensitivity in different regions of the body surface. Acta Physiologica Scandinavica **31**(2–3), 285–289 (1954). https://doi.org/10.1111/j.1748-1716.1954.tb01139.x
23. Yoo, Y., Yoo, T., Kong, J., Choi, S.: Emotional responses of tactile icons: effects of amplitude, frequency, duration, and envelope. In: 2015 IEEE World Haptics Conference (WHC) (2015). https://doi.org/10.1109/whc.2015.7177719

Design and Applications

The Reciprocity of Speculative and Product Design Research in an Industrial Framework

Claire Richards[1,2,3](✉), Nicolas Misdariis[2], and Roland Cahen[3]

[1] Actronika SAS, 75019 Paris, France
clairicha@gmail.com
[2] STMS-IRCAM-CNRS-SU-Ministère de la Culture, 75004 Paris, France
[3] Le Centre de Recherche en Design ENSCI Les Ateliers/ENS Paris-Saclay, 91190 Gif-sur-Yvette, France

Abstract. Wearable audio-tactile devices can be evaluated not only in terms of the perceptual experiences they elicit, but also how they come to exist. In this project case study, we show how the industrial environment influenced the design processes that have structured both the purpose and the form of two wearable audio-tactile devices, here described as design artifacts. We elaborate two design artifacts in terms of speculative and product design processes: the speculative design artifact (the multimodal harness) which was conceived to challenge the user's assumptions about hearing, and the product design artifact (Ryzm^{TM}) to bring the user an improved listening experience. In turn, we reveal the reciprocity of our speculative and product design processes: the creative interactions that bound the two artifacts' development created a connection between otherwise distinct scientific and commercial objectives.

Keywords: Wearable technology · Audio-tactile · Design research

1 Introduction

Our research centers on the creation and study of wearable audio-tactile devices, built to transmit vibrations that stimulate both the senses of touch and hearing. To better understand the potential for body-based listening and the compositional possibilities it affords, we focus on three main axes: the exploration of sensory capacities [1], wearable device design processes, and audio-tactile sensory effect composition [2]. Here, we focus on the second axis: understanding how design processes have shaped the purpose and form of two wearable audio-tactile devices, defined as design artifacts. Both of the artifacts manifest the main objective behind our research: push the possibilities for including more of the body in the listening experience. However, at the start of their development, the devices had contrasting purposes: one aimed for novel experimental possibilities, while the other centered on commercial applications.

© The Author(s), under exclusive license to Springer Nature Switzerland AG 2022
C. Saitis et al. (Eds.): HAID 2022, LNCS 13417, pp. 81–91, 2022.
https://doi.org/10.1007/978-3-031-15019-7_8

In this case study, we position these artifacts of our research in terms of speculative and product design. Our goal in categorizing our work and retrospectively evaluating these design processes is to demonstrate the value of coordinated scientific and commercial work, which has ultimately advanced our research objective and better integrated our project within its industrial environment.

2   Context and Motivations

2.1   Speculative and Product Design: What's the Difference?

Before we explain the approaches of speculative design and product design, we note that design research differs from pure scientific research: rather than focusing on *products* of an investigation, design research centers on the *process* of investigation itself [3]. In this paper, we explore the concrete outputs of our research in terms of the design processes that supported their creation.

In a nutshell, product design is about a project's targeted market, and speculative design the discourse surrounding it [4,5]. Product designers find creativity from within the "problem space", a working space confined by the constraints of the project's industrial environment: temporal, ergonomic, material, regulatory, etc. [4]. The product designer's goal is to draw a future product's path to the market, but an iterative problem-solving process of development and testing must first occur. With our industrial partner, Actronika, we have worked within these real-world constraints in order to find a practical application of our speculative research. The purpose of speculative design is to provoke thought and stimulate debate among designers and consumers by "exploring new aesthetic, functional and cultural possibilities for technology" [6]. Its approach allows us to consider both what we *do not* want and what we *do* want in our tech-infused future [7]. Speculative designs can appear impractical and idealistic because they live in a world with no marketplace constraints. Instead, they seek to expose alternatives and challenge the status quo of the things we build.

2.2   Related Research: State-of-the-Art

Before we detail our design artifacts, we'll first give some context and introduce some of the research in the auditory and tactile domains that informed their creation. The perceptual ranges and discriminatory limits of hearing and touch are compatible and overlapping. The skin's ability to interpret vibrotactile information can be broken down into several key characteristics of the presented stimulus: its frequency, intensity, duration, waveform and position on the body. These parameters of vibrotactile signal design have much in common with those of auditory signal design (pitch, amplitude, duration, timbre, spatialization), but the two senses do not process vibrations in the same way [8]. Opposed to auditory perception, which is centralized to the head, our tactile perception of vibrations is dispersed all over the surface of our body [9]. The tactile perception of vibrations in the frequency range between approximately 20–1000 Hz overlaps auditory sensitivity between 20–20 kHz. Despite differences in the two sensory organs' processing capacities, researchers have found that auditory stimulation can affect tactile perception [10,11], and vice versa [12].

Researchers and product designers have therefore naturally investigated the use of vibrotactile technology for augmented sensory experiences of sound by creating body-based interfaces. The "model human cochlea" system, integrated in an armchair-form tactile device called the Emoti-Chair, separates audio signals into frequency bands from 20–2500 Hz, displayed to the user via 16 voice-coil actuators, arranged in two vertical rows [13]. The Hapbeat and Vibeat were both designed to vibrate in time with music, worn as a necklace or bracelet [14,15]. The Soundshirt, originally designed for deaf individuals to experience philharmonic music, integrates 30 micro-actuators (type unspecified) in a thin, flexible garment [16]. The Soundshirt's frequency-based organization of tactile stimulations differentiates it from the Subpac, a vest that filters bass frequencies (5–125 Hz) from the audio of a connected device via two large voice coil actuators located on the back [17]. Finally, wearable devices such as the Soundbrenner Pulse and the Body:Suit:Score were developed as tactile musical aids, helping to keep time or follow the score [18,19]. Based alone on their varying dimensions of scale of development, context of use, and underlying theory, the above-listed devices also provide a diverse range of examples in speculative and product design. However, for the context of this paper, we restrict our analysis to a case study of our own research.

Inspired by the works listed above, we distinguish our audio-tactile device design based on how we employ vibration. We aim to elicit sound perception via extra-tympanic conduction (ETC) at specific sites on the human torso, paired with vibrotactile stimulation of the skin. Commonly described as bone conduction, we refer to contact-based sound transmission as "extra-tympanic", because there is speculation that soft tissue is involved in transmission mechanisms [20]. Notable past investigations of ETC are primarily based on the anatomy of the skull [21], but research has also shown the potential for sound perception via more distant sites of stimulation on the body such as the neck and back [20]. By testing the limits of ETC and the resulting tactile sensations elicited by vibratory stimulation, we explore the main objective of our research: build audio-tactile devices that challenge the common conception of sound perception and show that the body can be as much a part of listening as the ears.

3 Positioning Our Work in Design Processes

In this section, we will show how we manifested our research objective in the form of design artifacts. The artifact, a concrete output of a design process, serves as an interface "between an 'inner' environment, the substance and organisation of the artifact itself, and an 'outer' environment, the surroundings in which it operates" [3]. Building on this idea, in this section we will describe each design artifact first in terms of its surroundings (purpose) and substance (form). By detailing the purpose and form of each artifact, we position them within the processes of speculative and product design. Following this section, we will further illustrate the positive interactions between the two processes to demonstrate their reciprocity.

3.1 Speculative Design Artifact

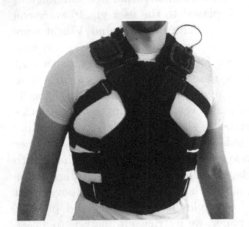 

Fig. 1. The multimodal harness. Nine voice-coil motors (Actronika HapCoil) are integrated in the wearable structure inside hard plastic modules on the clavicles, spine and ribs. The velcro straps tighten the modules' contact against the body, whose vibrations penetrate the body to elicit ETC sound perception, and stimulate the skin for tactile sensations. Users receive earplugs and a noise-reducing headset (3M Peltor X5A) in order to protect them from all external noises created by the actuators and ensure they hear only via ETC.

Speculative Artifact Purpose. The multimodal harness (see Fig. 1) was born from the motivation to challenge the status quo of listening experiences, one that assumes we need properly functioning ears to appreciate sound. This motive naturally led us to create an object that looks strange, even absurd. The notion of hearing through our skin and bones may also seem bizarre, but the multimodal harness makes this a real experience, while keeping it at arm's length from practical everyday use due to its inherent ergonomic constraints and cyborg aesthetic. Beyond its look, the experience of the multimodal harness is also an argument for its classification as speculative design. The act of putting on the harness requires the user to question their assumptions about sound perception. In order to hear, users must first become deaf: when using the harness, they cover their ears from all external, airborne sounds in order to ensure they are only hearing via extra-tympanic conduction. Instead of perceiving the sounds via one central point (the head), the user's torso is covered with vibrating modules that stimulate their skin, muscles, ligaments and bones. The harness is therefore a vessel for speculative debate, blurring the boundaries of auditory experiences.

By using initial interfaces for multimodal effect design, we can create sensory effects that support our hypothesized mode of listening: sounds reach the ears from within the body, paired with accompanying spatialized tactile sensations that expand, slide and dart across the outer skin's surface [2]. During demo sessions of these interfaces, users have commented that after an initial period of adjustment, they feel a rapid connection to their bodies, concentrating only on the sounds and sensations. In this direction of thought, the multimodal harness fits in an alternate timeline of our physical connection to sound... could we design interfaces to envelop our bodies in sound in the way that headphones envelop our heads?

Speculative Artifact Form. The multimodal harness is sci-fi-like in its appearance, its strange protruding structure inviting the user to expect an unusual sensory experience. We defined its form based on two key, albeit contradictory constraints: tight contact against the body, and user comfort. In order to optimize sound transmission and avoid signal attenuation, the point of contact with the body should be made of hard material, secured tightly against the user's body. Balancing good signal transmission and basic comfort therefore became a principal design challenge. We addressed this via the flexibility of the modules (see Fig. 2) and the ergonomic aspects of the harness structure, co-developed with costume design studio Les Vertugadins.

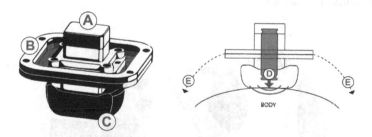

Fig. 2. The vibratory module. The module snaps onto extended fabric, tightened between the edges of the frame (B). A rounded, hard bottom (C) comes into contact with the body, transmitting the vibrations of the actuator to the user. The actuator's axis of vibration (D) is orthogonal to the body's surface. It "breathes" within its structural frame, and is pulled against the body by straps attached at all four corners (E).

The technical aspects of the module allow the wearable device to adapt to nine points of stimulation on the clavicles, ribs, and spine. Velcro straps are attached to all corners of the modules, pulling them against the body. The voice coil actuators are connected to a multichannel audio-haptic card (Actronika HSD

Mk-1). The card is wire-powered, and a USB audio port allows for wired connection to a computer for signal transmission. Our custom interfaces for audio-tactile effect composition are in a preliminary stage, and we need to conduct more perceptual research before we can fine-tune and calibrate the effects to the body's sensitivity [2]. The harness cannot be worn for long periods due to its skin-tight fit, so today's use is limited to experimentation and demonstration.

3.2   Product Design Artifact

Product Artifact Purpose. With Ryzm™, we bridge the gap between our ongoing scientific investigation and the tangible value of our work to our research partner, Actronika, a growing deep-tech business specialized in vibrotactile integration and product development. By adapting to this industrial context, we find ourselves in what is probably a common situation, as "the majority of design research is paid for by the development industry" [22]. To adapt, we identified a use case that fit our initial results and the company's haptic expertise: tactile-augmented listening experiences. Ryzm™ was imagined as a tactile listening device that will build on things consumers have already experienced about audio technology and haptic accessories, but in a slightly different way. To make new technology more easily acceptable, that degree of difference should sway users' perception of the product towards an improved existing experience rather than one that is totally new and unusual [23]. If successful, Ryzm™ may allow us to inject an aspect of our research into society at large, communicating that sensory experiences of sound are diverse and arguably under-served by today's dominant audio technology.

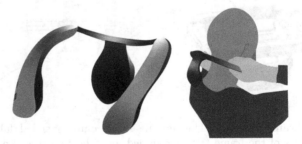

Fig. 3. The product design artifact. A preliminary illustration of the future Ryzm™ device, designed for tactile augmentation of listening. The device integrates three positions of vibrotactile stimulation on the upper neck and clavicles.

Product Artifact Form. We designed Ryzm™ in order to consolidate results from our prior research with simplified formal aspects of the multimodal harness (see Fig. 3). The device is to be worn around the neck, targeting three of the most sensitive positions for ETC as found in our prior psychophysical study [1].

On both clavicles and the upper neck, we integrate three voice-coil actuators to transmit the vibratory signals. Vibrations on both clavicles allow for stereo-type effects, and a third point of stimulation on the neck adds potential for tactile effect diversity. The vibratory effects could therefore make sound accessible to all hearing profiles, either via tactile stimulation or in combination with ETC. In contrast to the multimodal harness, Ryzm^{TM}'s future design will not require users to wear earplugs. To improve ease of use and comfort, this feature combined with other ergonomic aspects of the product (positioning on the body, tightness, number of actuators) will change the potential perceptual experiences in comparison to the multimodal harness. Future user testing with prototypes will help Actronika to prioritize key features and design better algorithms for audio signal transformation into vibratory stimuli, displayed by Ryzm^{TM}. We defined these features not only based on ergonomics and comfort, but also to draw comparison to existing products on the market: neck-worn speakers are now sold by prominent acoustic companies such as Bose[1] and Sony[2]. Future users' familiarity with such existing devices may ease the acceptance of Ryzm^{TM} as a product designed for listening, despite obvious formal differences from classic headsets.

4   Positive Project Impacts

Through a retrospective view on the artifacts' development, we can give a few insights about the complementarity of the speculative and product design processes. Their reciprocal nature can be demonstrated in terms of three main positive project impacts: it advanced a common objective, defined the product concept, and built mutual understanding between our commercial and scientific partners.

4.1   Positive Impact 1: Advancing a Common Objective

Though their purposes and forms are different, the process of creating the two design artifacts has taken our research objective in a common direction. The act of wearing the multimodal harness forces the user to challenge their assumptions about sound perception and helps to imagine another evolutionary path of personal listening devices. However, its speculative purpose constrains its use to experimentation: it is heavy, wired, requires the use of earplugs, and users can realistically wear it only for short periods of time due to the tight fit. Finding its roots in the same research objective, Ryzm^{TM} offers a compromise between idealism and practicality. The product concept suggests a more easily acceptable, ergonomic and less time-consuming solution to the industrial development of novel audio-tactile wearable technology. Such a product could already introduce ETC and tactile sensations of sound to the upper neck and clavicles, and potentially pave the way for more of the body in future listening devices.

---

[1] Bose SoundWear Companion speaker.
[2] Sony SRS-NS7 Wireless Neckband Speaker.

4.2   Positive Impact 2: Defining a Product Concept

In Fig. 4, we illustrate how the "problematic" nature of the speculative artifact helped define the product concept in terms of industrial considerations: the user, the scale of development, the market, and project timelines. We first identified the most impractical aspects of the multimodal harness to define Ryzm^{TM}'s future characteristics: uni-size, lightweight, simplified development and use, and familiar appearance. Without the multimodal harness at hand, we would not have had these points of comparison that helped guide the definition of a user-centered product.

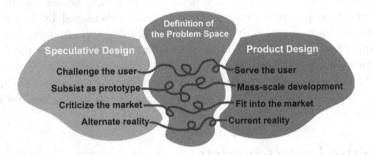

Fig. 4. In our project, the speculative design process influenced the product design process due to the problem space which naturally emerged between them. This problem space was built on contrasting purposes, as shown in the figure. The most "problematic" aspects of the multimodal harness revealed how Ryzm^{TM} must be different in order to be commercially practical.

4.3   Positive Impact 3: Fostering Mutual Understanding

Certain key moments in each artifacts' development demonstrate the interactions between the two design processes (see Fig. 5). To be able to respond to our industrial partner's commercial requirements for our project, we needed to understand their expectations and facilitate their understanding of our research: something best done through a collaborative activity. We therefore started the Ryzm^{TM} project during a workshop with colleagues. This resulted in an initial design concept, sketched while we finalized the first multimodal harness prototype. As we developed initial prototypes of the Ryzm^{TM} product, we also developed the second prototype of the harness. By developing the prototypes at the same time, we were able to maintain close contact with Actronika's mechanical and electronic design teams. Through our research, we also created another connection with Actronika's co-development partner, Les Vertugadins. The consistent internal communication and integration of our project in our partner's external network helped to assimilate the speculative research in the industrial context, building mutual understanding and accelerating both artifacts' development.

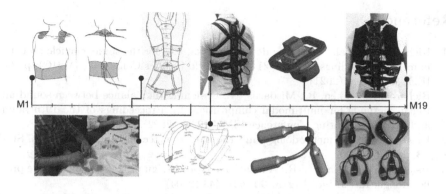

Fig. 5. Overlaid 19-month timeline of speculative (top) and product (bottom) artifact development. Images are taken from project records. The two processes overlap: phases of brainstorming, sketching and prototyping occurred in parallel and provided momentum for both artifacts' development.

5   Conclusion

Through all of these aspects of our case study, we demonstrate that the two parallel design processes had a reciprocal relationship: the interactions between them propelled both speculative and product development, and advanced our research in body-based listening experiences. The industrial environment that gave life to our work has helped to ground our speculative design approach and emphasize the importance of a practical output: an objective of commercial product design. The two design artifacts are interdependent despite their contrasting purposes: the scientific context for developing the multimodal harness could not have existed without the commercial context for developing Ryzm^{TM}, and vice versa. While speculative artifacts like the multimodal harness don't target commercial use, they give the design researcher the freedom of imagination. This creative liberty may seem to be at odds with the controlled nature of the scientific method and time-sensitive commercial development, but without it, neither design artifact would exist. Through this case study, we hope to have illustrated the value of a peaceful coexistence between uninhibited creativity (speculation) and practical constraint (commercialization) in an industrial environment. In future work, we will extend this analysis to other audio-tactile device development, with the hopes to expose commonalities and explore the diversity of speculative methods in multidisciplinary product design projects.

Acknowledgements. This research is part of a CIFRE industrial PhD contract, funded by Actronika SAS and the ANRT. We thank James Auger, Frédérique Pain and Pablo Arias for their contributions through insightful discussion. We also thank all of our colleagues and our co-development partner Les Vertugadins for their continued partnership.

References

1. Richards, C., et al.: Vibratory detection thresholds for the spine, clavicle and sternum. In: Proceedings of the 2021 IEEE World Haptics Conference (WHC), p. 346. IEEE, Montreal (2021)
2. Richards, C., Cahen, R., Misdariis, N.: Designing the balance between sound and touch: methods for multimodal composition. In: Proceedings of the 19th Sound and Music Computing Conference (SMC 2022) (2022)
3. Kroes, P.: Design methodology and the nature of technical artefacts. Des. Stud. **23**, 287–302 (2002)
4. Hsiao, S-W. and Chou, J-R.: A creativity-based design process for innovative product design. Int. J. Ind. Ergon. **34**, 421–443 (2004)
5. Dunne, A., Raby, F.: Design Noir: The Secret Life of Electronic Objects, p. 60. Birkhauser, Basel (2001)
6. Martin, H., Gaver, B.: Beyond the snapshot from speculation to prototypes in audiophotography. In: Proceedings of the 3rd Conference on Designing Interactive Systems: Processes, Practices, Methods, and Techniques (DIS 2000), Association for Computing Machinery, New York, NY, USA, pp. 55–65 (2000)
7. Auger, J.: Speculative design: crafting the speculation. Digit. Creativity **24**(1), 11–35 (2013)
8. Gunther, E., O'Modhrain, S.: Cutaneous grooves: composing for the sense of touch. J. New Music Res. **32**(4), 369–381 (2003)
9. Merchel, S., Altinsoy, M.E.: Psychophysical comparison of the auditory and vibrotactile perception: a survey. J. Multimodal User Interfaces **14**, 271–283 (2020)
10. Bresciani, J.P., et al.: Feeling what you hear: auditory signals can modulate tactile tap perception. Exp. Brain Res. **162**(2), 172–180 (2005)
11. Crommett, L.E., Pérez-Bellido, A., Yau, J.M.: Auditory adaptation improves tactile frequency perception. J. Neurophysiol. **117**(3), 1352–1362 (2017)
12. Schürmann, M., et al.: Touch activates human auditory cortex. Neuroimage **30**(4), 1325–1331 (2006)
13. Baijal, A. et al.: Composing vibrotactile music: a multi-sensory experience with the emoti-chair. In: IEEE Haptics Symposium (HAPTICS), pp. 509–515. IEEE, Vancouver (2012)
14. Hapbeat. https://hapbeat.com/index.html. Accessed 3 May 2022
15. Liron Gino designs Vibeat devices for deaf people to experience music. https://www.dezeen.com/2016/08/07/liron-gino-design-vibeat-listening-devices-wearable-hearing-impaired-tactile-music/. Accessed 3 May 2022
16. Soundshirt. https://cutecircuit.com/soundshirt/. Accessed 20 Apr 2022
17. Subpac. https://subpac.com/. Accessed 20 Apr 2022
18. Soundbrenner Pulse. https://www.soundbrenner.com/pulse/. Accessed 18 Apr 2022
19. West, T.J., et al.: The design of the Body:Suit:Score, a full-body vibrotactile musical score. In: Yamamoto, S., Mori, H. (eds) Human Interface and the Management of Information 2019, LNCS, vol. 11570, pp. 70–89. Springer, Cham (2019). https://doi.org/10.1007/978-3-030-22649-7-7
20. Adelman, C., et al.: Relation between body structure and hearing during soft tissue auditory stimulation. BioMed Res. Int. **2015**, 1–6 (2015)
21. Stenfelt, S., Goode, R.L.: Bone-conducted sound: physiological and clinical aspects. Otol. Neurotology **46**(12), 1245–1261 (2005)

22. Zimmerman, J., Forlizzi, J., Evenson, S.: Research through design as a method for interaction design research in HCI. In: Proceedings of the SIGCHI Conference on Human Factors in Computing Systems, CHI 2007, pp. 493–502
23. Desmet, P.M.A., Hekkert, P.: Framework of product experience. Int. J. Des. **1**(1), 57–66 (2007)

Designing Audio Feedback to Enhance Motion Perception in Virtual Reality

Francesco Soave[(✉)], Nick Bryan-Kinns, and Ildar Farkhatdinov

School of Electronic Engineering and Computer Science,
Queen Mary University of London, London, UK
f.soave@qmul.ac.uk

Abstract. We present our study on the design and evaluation of sound samples for motion perception in a Virtual Reality (VR) application. In previous study we found our sound samples to be incoherent with the VR visual channel. In current research we designed four new samples and tested them adapting standard subjective evaluation protocols to our needs. Twenty participants participated to the study and rated each animation in Realism, Matching and Plausibility. Significant differences were found among the sounds and discussion rose on the need for realism in VR applications as well as users' expectation and how it could influence their experience.

Keywords: Audio feedback · Virtual reality · Motion perception

1 Introduction and Background

In Virtual Reality (VR) applications, multisensoriality is an important part of the experience [3,34]. Research suggests using stimuli that go beyond the pure vision channel provides richer user experiences, improves task-related performances, reduces motion sickness and increases the complexity of the VR experience that we can build [10,21]. It is important to understand how our brain reacts to multimodal stimuli as the results of contrasting messages could easily break the illusion of the virtual world thus destroying the experience. For example if we're on a train looking outside the window our your brain couples the sounds and visual input of that specific moment in time. But if we were to take these two stimuli apart and only focus on sound, or apply that same audio to a different visual it is likely we'd receive conflicting stimuli. Studies on crossmodal correspondences have been carried out for over a century and it is well recognised that congruent stimuli that can be processed together by the human brain have positive effects on perceptual tasks [16,29,39]. Multimodal interactions were also recently confirmed in VR applications using both curved screens and Head Mounted Displays (HMDs) [15]. Even more important for

This work is supported by the EPSRC and AHRC Centre for Doctoral Training in Media and Arts Technology (EP/L01632X/1).

our context is that rich body of works focusing on motion perception in multisensory VR environments. These studies generally introduce both sound and haptic feedback in a VR application and results support the hypothesis that both stimuli improve participants' perceived motion as well as their user experience [3,8,14,22,26,32,41].

In our previous research [35–37] we built a multimodal VR setup which adds sound and vibrotactile haptic feedback to the visual channel of the environment. Haptics and sound are often studied together due to their intrinsic similarity: both stimuli can be produced by the same signal that is a sound wave. However often researchers on haptic feedback focused on design of predefined patterns of vibration that were not necessarily correlated with the audio [6,27].

Although the aim of our study was to investigate the role of multisensory stimulation on human perceptual ability towards motion, results revealed some incongruencies in the experiences, particularly between sound and vision. We subsequently began a design process to identify a coherent sound sample for our setup and drawing from existing literature in sound design research, we run a user study to determine how good or bad the connection of our sound samples was with the visual scene. In current research we describe our results in regards to three properties of the VR animation: "Realism" as in comparing to "real life" experience; "Matching" to identify coherency between 2 stimuli (vision and sound); "Plausibility" to gather participants opinion on the plausibility of the animation.

While properties like "Realism", "Presence" or "Immersion" are often measured in VR study by mean of standardised questionnaires [30,33,40] it is harder to choose a standard method for qualitative evaluation of audiovisual coherency of Virtual Environments (VEs) because of the plethora of protocols available. Examples of these protocols are the MOS (Mean Opinion Score), ACR rating scale, double blind and MUSHRA (MUltiple Stimuli with Hidden Reference and Anchor) [17,20,23,31]. For an extensive review of subjective evaluation methods in audiovisual setting we recommend [1,28]. Our approach therefore draws inspiration from experiments in sound design field and how researchers evaluate and compare different sound samples through perceptual measurements. We decided to apply the MUSHRA test protocol to our setup as it was successfully used before to explore realism of multiple audio tracks [18]. In this protocol there are usually multiple samples with two hidden audio files (reference and anchor). The reference represents the "perfect" sample and expected to always be rated maximum by the user. The anchor instead is at the opposite end of the scale and expected to always rank worst of all. These samples are introduced to help the user engage with the full range of evaluation scale. In subjective evaluation studies, input is generally provided by the user in the form of scales, often expressed through Likert scales [12,25]. Although several implementations of these scales (e.g. nominal, ordinal) have been studied in past (for an in depth discussion see [4]), researchers suggest that continuous sliders which shows the selected value and with the starting marker at the middle are to be preferred [2,9]. In this work, the three properties are evaluated with Likert scales in form of a 0–100 slider following literature's recommendations.

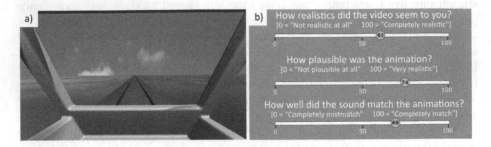

Fig. 1. a) The visual scene as seen from sitting inside the train in VR. On start, the idle train begins accelerating up to one of the three speed levels and the correspondent sound file is played. **b)** The evaluation scene where users interact with sliders to select a value for each property. The sliders were presented in random order after each animation.

2   Methodology

Animation Design. We designed a virtual scene of a person sitting on a train and moving linearly, depicted in Fig. 1a. Figure 1b shows the graphical user interface used for evaluation of the VR scene. The VR application was implemented in Unity 3D Games Engine and played through HMDs. The train is moving forward and accelerating constantly until the end of the trial. In each trial, the train accelerates up to one of three different speed levels identified in our previous work (50, 100 and 150 km/h). The four sounds (S_1–S_4) were designed with *FL Studio 20*, a Digital Audio Workstation (DAW) and produced by a mix of real train samples to accompany the VR scene (Fig. 2). The train sound samples were downloaded from freesound.org and edited according to the speed levels presented in each video. Each sound is made of two main samples: a "base" sound, which identifies the "rumble" of a moving train and an "accelerating" sample, which suggests the speed variation of the train. Each sample was 20 s in length and increasing linearly in frequency (to simulate acceleration) up to each trial's speed level. There were 12 sounds in total (three speed variations for each of the four sounds). One of the sounds (Sound 3) was designed to be the anchor and to perform worse than all others. Although literature suggests introducing a reference sound (better than all others) in our case this was not possible since we had no actual "real" reference video to compare the sounds to and simply attaching a realistic train sound to our animation was not effective, as verified in our previous study.

Experimental Protocol. The aim of the experiment was to identify an suitable sound sample to match the VR motion that can be used in future research. The

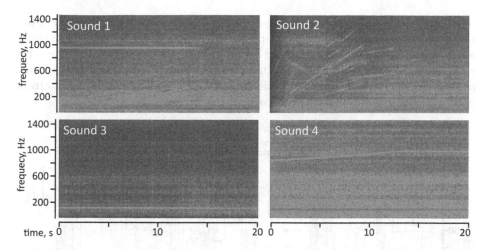

Fig. 2. Spectrograms of the sound files (window size 4096, 50% overlap, x4 oversampling). Main components are visible: low frequency engine rumble/noise and higher frequency accelerating pitch up to predefined speed. Sound 3 (anchor) clearly lacking pitch variation.

participants performed the study remotely and were not supervised. Encapsulated studies (i.e. remote and unsupervised) became common in the recent years [24]) and shown no particular issues in terms of quality of the data collected in remote setups [19,38]. They were recruited through Prolific platform and the requirements were to be at least 18 years old, not be diagnosed with epilepsy, to have normal or corrected to normal vision and to own a supported VR headset (Oculus Rift S, Oculus Quest or HTC Vive). Participants were given a text file with the instructions and visual instructions were provided during the test. There was no briefing at the end although they were asked to report any issue they might have encountered (none reported). The study was approved by our institution's Ethical Committee (QMERC20.133). After the demographic questions, each participant experienced 14 trials (two practice trials at the beginning) in random order. Each trial consisted of two parts: a 20 s animation of the train accelerating and its evaluation. The evaluation part was made of three horizontal sliders (in random order) to rate Realism, Matching, Plausibility by answering the questions as in Fig. 1b. At the end of all trials, they were presented with the animation they assigned the highest value (averaged across the three sliders) for each sound. They were asked to watch again these four animations and rank them based on which video was more realistic in terms of sound/visual matching. The protocol was initially piloted by researchers through a web survey on a 2D computer screen and subsequently turned into a VR application.

Participants. Twenty-two participants were recruited (13 males, 7 females; age distribution: 7 in the range 18–24 y.o., 11 in 25–34 y.o.; 1 in 35–44 y.o.; 1 in 45–54 y.o.). Six participants used VR equipment more than three times per week, six participants used it once per week and eight once per month. Three respondents did not play computer games; eight played less than three times per week and the remaining nine participants played games more than three times a week. Eleven participants reported no experience with sound design, five with very low experience, three with medium experience and only one participant has experience with sound design at professional level. The experimental data from two participant was removed from analysis due to errors in recording.

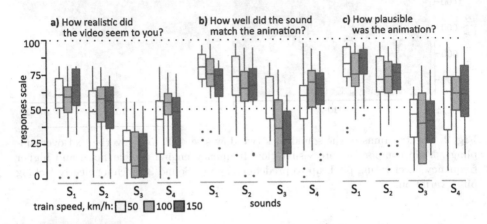

Fig. 3. a) Realism ratings for each sound and each speed level. **b)** Match ratings for each sound and each speed level. **c)** Plausibility ratings for each sound and each speed level. S_1, S_2, S_3 and S_4 correspond to Sounds 1–4, respectively.

3 Results

Figure 3 shows that higher values were assigned to Sound 1 and Sound 2 for all three questions, although it is not clear which one is the highest overall. Sound 3 performed badly and worse than all others, as expected since it was the anchor sample; its medians did not scored above 50% except for matching in 50 km/h speed level. Sound 4 performed better than Sound 3 but still below Sound 1 and Sound 2 in most cases. In general, realism values seem to be lower than matching and plausibility and this perhaps could be a consequence of not having a reference animation for the upper bound of the scale.

Kruskal Wallis test showed significance between sounds for the *Realism*, *Plausibility* and *Matching* scores. Posthoc Dunn Test (Bonferroni correction) was carried out and results are summarised in Table 1. The analysis confirms results of the plots, always reaching significance between Sound 3 and the other samples. Significant difference is not found between Sound 1 and 2. Finally, sound 4 is significantly different from Sound 1 and 3 but not from Sound 2.

Although we were not able to identify significance between Sound 1 and 2, Table 2 summarised the ranking that participants had to undertake at the end of the study. They were presented with the 4 animations they rated the highest

Table 1. Post hoc Dunn Test (Bonferroni corrected) results. Pairwise comparison to highlight which sounds are statistically different for the three properties (ns >1, <0.1, *<0.05, **<0.01, ***<0.001). S_1, S_2, S_3 and S_4 correspond to Sounds 1–4.

	Realism			Matching			Plausibility		
	S_1	S_2	S_3	S_1	S_2	S_3	S_1	S_2	S_3
Sound 2	ns			ns			ns		
Sound 3	***	***		***	***		***	***	
Sound 4	**	ns	***	***	*	**	**	ns	**

during the study trials (1 for each audio sample) and asked to experience them again and rank them. Results show a preference for Sound 1 which was ranked in first position by 11 participants. The same number of participants put Sound 3 in the lowest rank (4).

Table 2. Ranking of the four highest scoring animations (1 for each sound) for each participant. Each number is how many times that sound was put in that rank. Bold numbers are the highest count.

	Rank 1	Rank 2	Rank 3	Rank 4
Sound 1	**11**	5	2	2
Sound 2	7	**9**	1	3
Sound 3	1	4	4	**11**
Sound 4	1	2	**13**	4

Once identified Sound 1 as the more suitable sample we look for any significant differences between speed levels. Kruskal-Wallis test was conducted to examine the differences on the three properties according to the speed levels. No significant differences were found (Realism: $\chi^2 = 1.68$, $p = 0.43$, $df = 2$, Matching: $\chi^2 = 3.09$, $p = 0.21$, $df = 2$, Plausibility: $\chi^2 = 1.81$, $p = 0.40$, $df = 2$) therefore we cannot reject the null hypothesis and determine statistical differences between speed levels. We conclude that Sound 1 is equally suitable for each speed level.

4 Discussion

Through our user study we were able to identify Sound 1 as the more suitable for our train animation in Virtual Reality. We summarise considerations that rose from both the design process and the study results.

Realism as a property might not be relevant for a non-realistic application. If we aim for a realistic representation of a train's sound, choosing one sample over another might not just be a technical discussion but rather influenced from the context of our application (e.g. training simulation or a game), the target user (e.g. a game for infants of adults) and the chosen reference (i.e. for instance we might decide that our application uses a train of a specific country or in a set time period). Virtual Reality technology is used for training in various setups including medical, aviation, driving [5,11,13,43]. In that context it is important to produce a "realistic as possible" environment and to do so, researchers often adopt multisensory stimulation to recreate real-world experiences [42]. On the other hand in a gaming application it is likely that a realistic sound might produce the opposite effect, breaking the illusion or resulting in less exciting experience. We should therefore always consider the context in which a VR applications is produced and how this will influence the users.

The Role of Previous Experience and Expectation. The expectation of how a train should sound might influence one's judgement. Each train likely has a sound highly different from any other and this is due to various factors such as the rail tracks or the age of the carriage. If we are asked to imagine the sound of a train it is likely we imagine different things such as a steam locomotive or a high speed train. However it's likely an actual train's sound doesn't actually resemble either, especially from the passenger perspective. Modern high speed trains don't have any recognizable sound for a passenger, and often there is nothing in the audio domain that suggests acceleration or deceleration of the carriage (i.e. the sound is the same when train is idle, accelerating or steadily moving).

Background Sound. When sitting on a train, passengers don't normally focus on its sound and/or it's very hard to be in a quiet enough place to listen to it. Often there are other background sounds (e.g. announcements, other passengers). A distinction can be made between conscious and subconscious sounds as described in [7]. The first group mostly concerns speech sounds while the latter, also called ambient sounds, refer to audio that we may not process consciously but which still shapes our environment and feeling of immersion. Once again because of the influence background sound can have on the user experience it is important to evaluate the context of the application and determine the level of realism we want to achieve as it could be detrimental to VR properties such as immersion or presence.

5   Conclusion

This paper summarises the research we conducted to design and evaluate a set of sound samples to use in our Virtual Reality application. Starting from feedback received in our previous user study we designed four audio samples and conducted an experiment to determine which audio is more coherent with our visual animation. To do so we identified three main properties: Realism, Matching and Plausibility. We asked users to rate each VR scene in terms of these aspects and were able to select one sound sample. The protocol was based on standard audio evaluation methods and adapted to our needs. Several interesting aspects rose from the design process which highlight the importance of users' previous experience and expectations that should be considered when designing a VR application. Possible limitations of current study are related to lack of investigation in users' previous experience with train. It is possible that experienced travellers might respond differently because of a broader reference background. Another limitation could be related to the properties we identified. An extended survey might be carried out in future to expand to other keywords such as "Authenticity", "Believability", "Preference" and "Engagement" (i.e. dull or captivating) to identify possible correlation or contrast among various properties.

References

1. Bech, S., Zacharov, N.: Perceptual Audio Evaluation-Theory, Method and Application: Bech/Perceptual Audio Evaluation-Theory, Method and Application. Wiley, Chichester (2006)
2. Bosch, O.J., Revilla, M., DeCastellarnau, A., Weber, W.: Measurement reliability, validity, and quality of slider versus radio button scales in an online probability-based panel in Norway. Soc. Sci. Comput. Rev. **37**(1), 119–132 (2019)
3. Campos, J., Nusseck, H., Wallraven, C., Mohler, B., Bülthoff, H.: Visualization and (mis)perceptions in virtual reality. In: 10. Workshop Sichtsysteme: Visualisierung in der Simulationstechnik, pp. 10–14. Shaker (2007)
4. Carifio, J., Perla, R.J.: Ten common misunderstandings, misconceptions, persistent myths and urban legends about Likert scales and Likert response formats and their antidotes. J. Soc. Sci. **3**(3), 106–116 (2007)
5. Clifford, R.M., Jung, S., Hoermann, S., Billinghurst, M., Lindeman, R.W.: Creating a stressful decision making environment for aerial firefighter training in virtual reality. In: 2019 IEEE Conference on Virtual Reality and 3D User Interfaces (VR), pp. 181–189. IEEE, Osaka, March 2019
6. Dijk, E.O., Weffers-Albu, A., De Zeeuw, T.: A tactile actuation blanket to intensify movie experiences with personalised tactile effects. In: Demonstration Papers Proceedings 3rd International Conference on Intelligent Technologies for Interactive Entertainment (2009)
7. Dionisio, J.D.N., Iii, W.G.B., Gilbert, R.: 3D virtual worlds and the metaverse: current status and future possibilities. ACM Comput. Surv. **45**(3), 1–38 (2013)
8. Farkhatdinov, I., Ouarti, N., Hayward, V.: Vibrotactile inputs to the feet can modulate vection. In: 2013 World Haptics Conference (WHC), pp. 677–681. IEEE (2013)
9. Funke, F.: A web experiment showing negative effects of slider scales compared to visual analogue scales and radio button scales. Soc. Sci. Comput. Rev. **34**(2), 244–254 (2016)
10. Grassini, S., Laumann, K., de Martin Topranin, V., Thorp, S.: Evaluating the effect of multi-sensory stimulations on simulator sickness and sense of presence during HMD-mediated VR experience. Ergonomics **64**(12), 1532–1542 (2021)
11. Harrington, C.M., et al.: Development and evaluation of a trauma decision-making simulator in Oculus virtual reality. Am. J. Surg. **215**(1), 42–47 (2018)
12. Joshi, A., Kale, S., Chandel, S., Pal, D.: Likert scale: explored and explained. Br. J. Appl. Sci. Technol. **7**(4), 396–403 (2015)

13. Kemeny, A.: From driving simulation to virtual reality. In: Proceedings of the 2014 Virtual Reality International Conference, pp. 1–5. ACM, Laval, April 2014
14. Keshavarz, B., Campos, J.L., Berti, S.: Vection lies in the brain of the beholder: EEG parameters as an objective measurement of vection. Front. Psychol. **6**, 1581 (2015)
15. Malpica, S., Serrano, A., Allue, M., Bedia, M.G., Masia, B.: Crossmodal perception in virtual reality. Multimedia Tools Appl. **79**, 3311–3331 (2019)
16. Miller, J.: Channel interaction and the redundant-targets effect in bimodal divided attention. J. Exp. Psychol. **17**(1), 10 (1991)
17. Moffat, D., Reiss, J.D.: Objective evaluations of synthesised environmental sounds. In: Proceedings of the 21st International Conference on Digital Audio Effects (DAFx 2018), Aveiro, Portugal, 4–8 September 2018, p. 8 (2018)
18. Moffat, D., Reiss, J.D.: Perceptual evaluation of synthesized sound effects. ACM Trans. Appl. Percept. **15**(2), 1–19 (2018)
19. Mottelson, A., Hornbæk, K.: Virtual reality studies outside the laboratory. In: Proceedings of the 23rd ACM Symposium on Virtual Reality Software and Technology, pp. 1–10. ACM, Gothenburg, November 2017
20. Neuendorf, M., Nagel, F.: Exploratory studies on perceptual stationarity in listening test-part I: real world signals from custom listening tests. In: Audio Engineering Society Convention, vol. 131. Audio Engineering Society (2011)
21. Ng, A.K.T., Chan, L.K.Y., Lau, H.Y.K.: A study of cybersickness and sensory conflict theory using a motion-coupled virtual reality system. In: 2018 IEEE Conference on Virtual Reality and 3D User Interfaces, March 2018
22. Nilsson, N.C., Nordahl, R., Sikström, E., Turchet, L., Serafin, S.: Haptically induced illusory self-motion and the influence of context of motion. In: Isokoski, P., Springare, J. (eds.) EuroHaptics 2012. LNCS, vol. 7282, pp. 349–360. Springer, Heidelberg (2012). https://doi.org/10.1007/978-3-642-31401-8_32
23. Pinson, M.H., et al.: The influence of subjects and environment on audiovisual subjective tests: an international study. IEEE J. Sel. Top. Sig. Process. **6**(6), 640–651 (2012)
24. Ratcliffe, J., Soave, F., Bryan-Kinns, N., Tokarchuk, L., Farkhatdinov, I.: Extended Reality (XR) remote research: a survey of drawbacks and opportunities. In: Proceedings of the 2021 CHI Conference on Human Factors in Computing Systems, pp. 1–13. ACM, Yokohama, May 2021
25. Likert, R.: A technique for the measurement of attitudes. Arch. Psychol. **22**, 5–55 (1932)
26. Riecke, B.E., Feuereissen, D., Rieser, J.J.: Auditory self-motion illusions ("circular vection") can be facilitated by vibrations and the potential for actual motion. In: Proceedings of the 5th Symposium on Applied Perception in Graphics and Visualization - APGV 2008, p. 147. ACM Press, Los Angeles (2008)
27. Riecke, B.E., Feuereissen, D., Rieser, J.J.: Auditory self-motion simulation is facilitated by haptic and vibrational cues suggesting the possibility of actual motion. ACM Trans. Appl. Percept. **6**(3), 1–22 (2009)
28. Lipshitz, S., Vanderkooy, J.: The great debate: subjective evaluation. J. Audio Eng. Soc. **29**, 482–491 (1980)
29. Sapir, E.: A study in phonetic symbolism. J. Exp. Psychol. **12**(3), 225–239 (1929)
30. Schwind, V., Knierim, P., Haas, N., Henze, N.: Using presence questionnaires in virtual reality. In: Proceedings of the 2019 CHI Conference on Human Factors in Computing Systems - CHI 2019, pp. 1–12. ACM Press, Glasgow (2019)

31. Selfridge, R., Moffat, D., Reiss, J.D.: Physically derived sound synthesis model of a propeller. In: Proceedings of the 12th International Audio Mostly Conference on Augmented and Participatory Sound and Music Experiences. ACM, August 2017
32. Seya, Y., Shinoda, H.: Relationship between vection and motion perception in depth. Attention Percept. Psychophys. **80**(8), 2008–2021 (2018). https://doi.org/10.3758/s13414-018-1567-y
33. Slater, M., Usoh, M.: Presence in immersive virtual environments. In: Proceedings of IEEE Virtual Reality, pp. 90–96. IEEE, Seattle (1993)
34. Slater, M., Sanchez-Vives, M.V.: Enhancing our lives with immersive virtual reality. Front. Rob. AI **3**, 74 (2016)
35. Soave, F., Bryan-Kinns, N., Farkhatdinov, I.: A preliminary study on full-body haptic stimulation on modulating self-motion perception in virtual reality. In: De Paolis, L.T., Bourdot, P. (eds.) AVR 2020. LNCS, vol. 12242, pp. 461–469. Springer, Cham (2020). https://doi.org/10.1007/978-3-030-58465-8_34
36. Soave, F., Farkhatdinov, I., Bryan-Kinns, N.: Multisensory teleportation in virtual reality applications. In: 2021 IEEE Conference on Virtual Reality and 3D User Interfaces Abstracts and Workshops (VRW), pp. 377–379. IEEE (2021)
37. Soave, F., Padma Kumar, A., Bryan-Kinns, N., Farkhatdinov, I.: Exploring terminology for perception of motion in virtual reality. In: Designing Interactive Systems Conference 2021, pp. 171–179 (2021)
38. Steed, A., Frlston, S., Lopez, M.M., Drummond, J., Pan, Y., Swapp, D.: An 'In the Wild' experiment on presence and embodiment using consumer virtual reality equipment. IEEE Trans. Vis. Comput. Graph. **22**(4), 1406–1414 (2016)
39. Stevens, J.C., Marks, L.E.: Cross-modality matching of brightness and loudness. Proc. Natl. Acad. Sci. **54**(2), 407–411 (1965)
40. Usoh, M., Catena, E., Arman, S., Slater, M.: Using presence questionnaires in reality. Presence Teleoperators Virtual Environ. **9**(5), 497–503 (2000)
41. Väljamäe, A., Larsson, P., Västfjäll, D., Kleiner, M.: Vibrotactile enhancement of auditory-induced self-motion and spatial presence. J. Audio Eng. Soc. **54**(10), 954–963 (2006)
42. Weidner, F., Hoesch, A., Poeschl, S., Broll, W.: Comparing VR and non-VR driving simulations: an experimental user study. In: 2017 IEEE Virtual Reality (VR), pp. 281–282. IEEE, Los Angeles (2017)
43. Wu, E., Perteneder, F., Koike, H., Nozawa, T.: How to VizSki: visualizing captured skier motion in a VR Ski training simulator. In: The 17th International Conference on Virtual-Reality Continuum and its Applications in Industry, pp. 1–9. ACM, Brisbane, November 2019

Using Audio Recordings to Characterise a Soft Haptic Joystick

Joshua P. Brown[✉] and Ildar Farkhatdinov

Queen Mary University of London, London, UK
{j.p.brown,i.farkhatdinov@qmul.ac.uk}

Abstract. The principle of particle jamming, a physical effect where fluids can be made to change their hardness at will, has many applications in engineering. Previous research has investigated combining this change of hardness with other haptic effects, resulting in a technology that can render vibration, hardness/softness and shape. This paper proceeds to describe the application of this technology to a soft haptic joystick handle for use in interactive games and telerobotics scenarios. Dynamically generated sound waveforms are used to drive vibrations inside the handle, and a microphone records these as they reach the tip of the handle under different jamming conditions. Audio frequency analysis is then used to analyse the behaviour of the resulting vibrations.

This analysis shows that vibration is lowest under a strong vacuum, confirming previous observations that increasing the hardness of the particle fluid has the effect of restricting the displacement of the source vibrations. Moreover, frequency of vibration remained broadly stable in both hard and soft states again confirming previous observations. These results, obtained with a fundamentally different haptic device and sound-based instrumentation, necessitate the conclusion that the behaviour of particle jamming controlled vibration is repeatable and controllable regardless of the physical configuration in which it is used.

Keywords: Soft haptics · Particle jamming · Vibration

1 Introduction

Particle jamming refers to the principle of using controlled air pressure to affect the viscosity of a granular fluid inside a soft, sealed container [2]. This can be used to create shape-changing [6], shape-memory [8] and hardness changing [7] haptic interfaces.

These previously complex haptic sensations have applications in a variety of fields. In virtual reality, soft hatic devices can be worn to provide haptic feedback naturally to different parts of the body [1,9,11]. In telerobotics, particle jamming can be integrated into interactive devices [3] where changes of hardness have been shown to be useful to relay environmental information to users of remote robots [10].

© The Author(s), under exclusive license to Springer Nature Switzerland AG 2022
C. Saitis et al. (Eds.): HAID 2022, LNCS 13417, pp. 102–111, 2022.
https://doi.org/10.1007/978-3-031-15019-7_10

Previous work has added rendering of vibrotactile sensations to a haptic surface based on particle jamming [4,5]. This design is now extended and expanded with the intention of creating a haptic system that can be retrofitted to a computer joystick or other interactive devices to render a wide variety of haptic sensations whilst controlling a remote mobile robot.

In what follows, particle jamming technology is employed to create a joystick handle which offers three distinct modes of haptic sensation - vibration, hardness/softness change and shape change. The behaviour of this device is then characterised using an electret microphone to determine how hardness and vibration interact in order to inform the design of haptic feedback delivered through the handle.

2 Soft Haptic Joystick Based on Particle Jamming

An obvious target for integrating the particle jamming system is a computer joystick. This is already a ubiquitous interface in many HCI and HRI contexts such as computer gaming and robot teleoperation, which will accelerate the process of evaluating the benefits of multimodal haptic feedback in a variety of application domains. A prototype multimodal haptic joystick handle was therefore created to demonstrate and allow experimental evaluation of these applications (Fig. 1b). The simple handle shape associated with a joystick also allows the prototype device to serve as a template for integrating the underlying technology into other devices, thus speeding up prototyping.

2.1 Functional Design

The hardness or softness of the handle are controlled by the particle jamming effect. Here, negative air pressure can be used to deform the silicone handle causing the particle fluid to jam. The lower the pressure, the stronger this effect and the harder the handle is to the touch. As the handle contains two solid LRAs, there is a limit to the softness that can be achieved. Unlike in some soft-haptic devices however, this is actually beneficial as it preserves the device's straight, handle shape which is important when the joystick is used as an input device and has to be pushed in a specific direction.

Vibrotactile sensations are generated by a pair of Actronika HapCoil One Linear Resonant Actuators (LRAs), controlled by an Actronika HSD mk.1 high current sound card. Previous research has shown that the vibrotactile effect can be modulated by the particle jamming system as well as by direct signal control of the actuators [5].

Finally, air pressure above atmospheric levels can be used to inflate the device, causing the handle to change shape. In the user's hand, this will cause the device to exert a force on the inside of the palm. The handle geometry is designed to increase in diameter more readily than length during inflation, as this is more likely to be felt during conventional, one-handed operation. Alternative geometries could promote expansion in other directions, such as in length

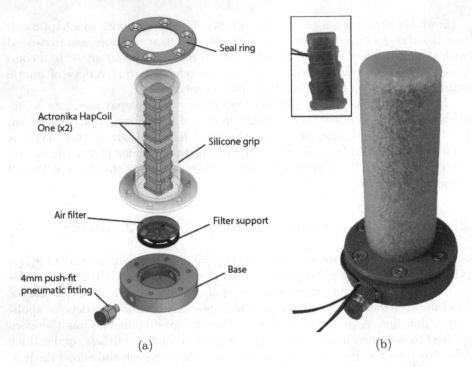

Fig. 1. (a) Exploded CAD model showing the construction of the multimodal haptic joystick. (b) Figure: the prototype joystick. Insert: the Actronika HapCoil One LRA with ribbed enclosure.

but not diameter to lift the thumb if it were to be left resting on the top of the handle, or to inflate the whole of the handle uniformly. These effects can be achieved by thickening the silicone in different areas of the handle wall.

2.2 Physical Design

The joystick consists of a 3D printed silicone handle (Formlabs Elastic resin, 50A shore durometer) which is clamped to a 3D printed plastic base. The base provides access for pneumatic hoses via a 4mm push-fit connector and electrical cables as well as allowing the joystick handle to be mounted to other devices, such as a flight stick base or force feedback interface. The silicone handle measures 100mm in length, 35mm in diameter and has a wall thickness of 1mm which is sufficiently thick to mask the texture of the particle fluid whilst still being thin enough to deform and exert pressure to jam the particles under vacuum. The top wall of the grip is much thicker (3mm) in order to maintain the overall cylindrical shape of the handle under changing air pressure.

The handle is filled with the particle fluid for jamming (quinoa seeds of approx 1mm dia) and the two LRAs. The LRAs are themselves encapsulated within ribbed sleeves (Fig. 1b insert) which serve to both prevent seeds from entering the actuators and agitate the particles during vibration (Fig. 1a). A cotton filter, reinforced with a plastic frame, keeps the particle fluid contained within the handle and provides a pass-through for four wires which control the two LRAs. The complete assembly (not including the particle fluid) is shown in Fig. 1a.

There are four threaded holes on the underside of the base to allow the joystick to be attached to a variety of interactive computer input and force feedback devices.

2.3 Operation

The joystick handle is controlled by a Raspberry Pi 3 Model B+. This dynamically generates audio signals in real time, allowing any sound waveform to be manipulated and played through the LRAs. These audio samples are output to an Actronika HSD mk.1 20-channel, high current sound card to control vibration. Air pressure is controlled via two MCP4725 DAC modules which are then amplified by op-amp circuits to achieve a range from 0-10VDC and sent as input to pneumatic regulators. Negative pressure is controlled by an SMC Pneumatics ITV0090-3BS regulator, whilst positive pressure is controlled by an ITV0050-3BS regulator (not used in this study). Feedback from the pressure sensors is collected by a Texas Instruments ADS1263 10-channel ADC.

3 Experimental Characterisation

Whilst the behaviour of the underlying particle jamming technology has previously been explored, it is useful to verify that the behaviour demonstrated in 2020 [5] remains valid in a device with a fundamentally different configuraton. Here, vibration is provided in one direction using a linear resonant actuator, whilst previous characterisation of the technology has used a two dimensional ERM (Eccentric Rotating Mass) motor. Moreover, the particle volume in this device is significantly lower, and the particle fluid is contained within an almost entirely soft enclosure, rather than the predominantly rigid enclosure used in the aforementioned study.

3.1 Experiment Design and Apparatus

An experiment has been designed to explore the effect of pressure control on vibration propagation up the soft handle. The joystick was placed on a foam pad and a highly sensitive electret condenser microphone (Knowles VEK-H-30108-000) was glued to the top of the joystick handle to measure on-axis vibration (the only axis in which vibrations are expected to be felt). A $1\mu F$ capacitor was connected in series with the optput to correct for DC bias. The microphone signal was then recorded at 48 KHz on an Apple MacBook Pro. The LRAs were driven with 15 Hz sine wave and the vibration was recorded in both the hard state (−100 KPa vacuum) and soft state (atmospheric pressure). In each state, vibrations were also recorded with and without a user's hand gently grasping the joystick. In each trial, the whole surface of the user's palm and fingers gripped the shaft of the joystick firmly, but not so hard as to change the shape of the shaft to conform to the user's fist. This gives rise to 4 experimental conditions:

- S: Soft state
- SG: Soft state, one hand grasping the joystick
- H: Hard state
- HG: Hard state, one hand grasping the joystick

Each condition was recorded for 10 s and the outputs checked for anomalies or decay in amplitude, frequency and shape, which were not present in any of the recordings. After recording, a Fourier analysis was conducted on each recording to determine the frequency of vibrations passed up the handle and whether this was affected by the particle jamming. Several cycles of vibration in each condition were also extracted to provide an understanding of the shape of the output vibration.

Additionally, two recordings of ambient noise were made for comparison with the vibration recordings - one with and one without the vacuum pump operating. These additional recordings were analysed in the same way as the conditions described above. The noteworthy results are presented below.

3.2   Ambient Noise

Ambient noise was measured with a maximum peak-peak signal amplitude (digital sound level) of $\pm 4\mathrm{e}16$ (Fig. 2). Powering on the vacuum pump increased this by almost a factor of 5 to a much more uniform level of $\pm 1.9\mathrm{e}17$ (Fig. 2).

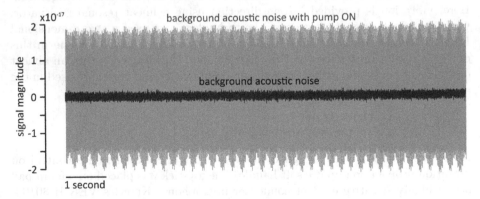

Fig. 2. Ambient noise recorded during the experiment with and without the vacuum pump operating.

Fourier analysis showed that there is no significant periodicity to the ambient noise, meaning that the joystick was sufficiently well isolated from background vibrations during the experiment (Fig. 3a). The vacuum pump introduced a peak 100 Hz (Fig. 3b), which can be disregarded from the results for the hard conditions.

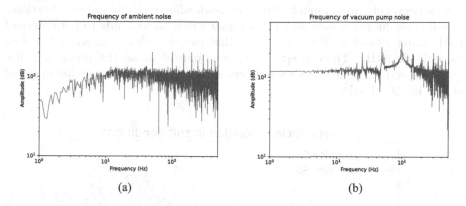

(a)   (b)

Fig. 3. (a) Frequency of ambient noise during the experiment. (b) Frequency of vacuum pump noise during the experiment.

3.3   Soft State Vibration (conditions S and SG)

The S and SG conditions will be analysed together since it is useful to explore how the hardness state of the particle fluid affects the vibration response both with and without a user grasping the handle.

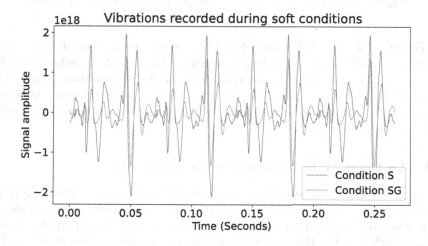

Fig. 4. Several vibration cycles recorded under soft jamming conditions S and SG.

In the S condition, the vibrations were recorded with a peak signal amplitude of approximately 2e18. This is two orders of magnitude above the ambient level shown above. A close-up view of the recorded signal shows a broadly periodic pattern of high and low amplitude oscillations (Fig. 4). The changes in amplitude have a period of approximately 0.07 s, corresponding to 15 Hz source vibrations. There is significant distortion to this signal which corresponds to harmonics of 15 Hz input vibration. We hypothesize that the joystick design resonates close to or 75 Hz 90 Hz. These frequencies are dominant in all the proceeding frequency spectra. The SG condition differs in magnitude, with a maximum signal amplitude of ±1.5e18.

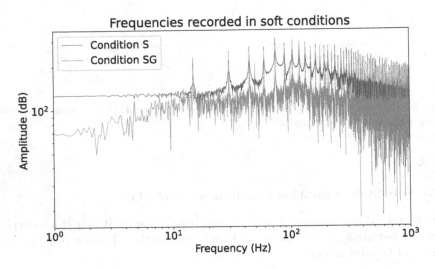

Fig. 5. Frequencies recorded under soft jamming conditions S and SG.

Fourier analysis of the whole of each recording goes further, demonstrating a frequency shift between the two conditions. Condition S records a peak frequency of 75 Hz, whereas the peak component of the SG condition 105 Hz. This is in fact much higher than 15 Hz source vibration, suggesting that transmission through the particle fluid caused very significant distortion of the original vibration pattern (Fig. 5).

3.4   Hard State Vibration (conditions H and HG)

In the H condition, vibration was measured with a maximum signal amplitude of ±1.3e18. The signal recorded is a relatively smooth sinusoid with periodically decreasing amplitude. This amplitude decrease shows strong periodicity with 15 Hz, which matches the source vibrations. The recording from condition HG has a maximum signal amplitude of 6.5e17, which is approximately half the amplitude of vibrations when not gripped. There is considerable distortion to the signal, as was observed in condition SG. The reduction in signal amplitude has the same overall frequency as in the H condition (Fig. 6).

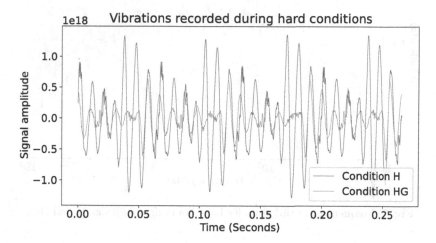

Fig. 6. Several vibration cycles recorded under hard jamming conditions H and HG.

The frequency spectrum shows that both hard conditions H and HG peak 105 Hz, with similar second peaks 90 Hz. The amplitude of components for HG are expectedly much lower than for H (Fig. 7).

4 Summary, Discussion and Future Work

From these results, a number of conclusions can be drawn. Firstly, vibration amplitude was highest in the soft conditions, indicating that a harder particle fluid limits the displacement of the actuators, damping the vibrations passed to the touch surface. Secondly, it was shown that a hand grasping the handle reduced the vibration amplitude further still, which is an important considera-tion for interactive devices which must be designed to be touched and manipu-lated by users. Finally, frequency of vibrations remained broadly in the range of 90-105Hz in all conditions.

These results confirm prior research into the effect of particle jamming on vibration. This is an important outcome, since the configuration of the joystick handle is fundamentally different to the experimental setup that has been used for characterisation in the past. This means that the behaviours described above and in the previous study can be confidently attributed to the underlying tech-nology rather than any feature of the specific implementation.

Future research will investigate the pshcyophysical effects of the different sen-sations generated by the handle, both alone and in combination. In the immedi-ate term, vibration will be used to try to create a sensation of movement of the

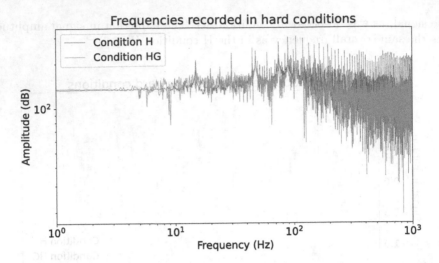

Fig. 7. Frequencies recorded under hard jamming conditions H and HG.

user's hand, as this effect has clear applications to telerobotics and VR. Additionally, it is hoped that the change of hardness may serve to strengthen the effect of force feedback against the user's hand or wrist and this interaction will be studied.

The handle will also be incorporated into existing HCI devices such as a computer joystick (Logitech 3D Pro joystick) or force feedback device (Human Robotix HRX-1 wrist interface) in order to enable a broader range of sensory studies, as well as application testing in telerobotics and computer gaming scenarios.

References

1. Al Maimani, A., Roudaut, A.: Frozen Suit: towarda Changeable Stiffness Suit and its Application for Haptic Games. In: Proceedings of the 2017 CHI Conference on Human Factors in Computing Systems, vol. 2017-May, pp. 2440–2448. ACM, New York, NY, USA, May 2017
2. Biroli, G.: A new kind of phase transition? Nature Phys. **3**, 222–223 (2007)
3. Brown, J., Farkhatdinov, I.: A Soft, vibrotactile, shape-changing joystick for Telerobotics. In: 2021 IEEE World Haptics Conference (WHC), pp. 1158–1158. IEEE, July 2021
4. Brown, J., Farkhatdinov, I.: Shape-changing touch pad based on particle jamming and vibration. In: 2021 IEEE World Haptics Conference (WHC), pp. 337–337. IEEE (2021)
5. Brown, J.P., Farkhatdinov, I.: Soft haptic interface based on vibration and particle jamming. In: IEEE Haptics Symposium, HAPTICS, vol. 2020-March, pp. 1–6. IEEE, Washington DC, March 2020
6. Follmer, S., Leithinger, D., Olwal, A., Cheng, N., Ishii, H.: Jamming user interfaces: programmable particle stiffness and sensing for malleable and shape-changing

devices. In: UIST 2012 - Proceedings of the 25th Annual ACM Symposium on User Interface Software and Technology, pp. 519–528 (2012)

7. Li, M., et al.: Multi-fingered haptic palpation utilizing granular jamming stiffness feedback actuators smart mater. Struct **23**, 95007 (2014)

8. Sato, T., Pardomuan, J., Matoba, Y., Koike, H.: ClaytricSurface: an interactive deformable display with dynamic stiffness control. IEEE Comput. Graph. Appl. **34**(3), 59–67 (2014)

9. Simon, T.M., Smith, R.T., Thomas, B.H.: Wearable jamming mitten for virtual environment haptics. In: International Symposium on Wearable Computers, pp. 67–70. ACM, Washington (2014)

10. Stanley, A.A., Mayhew, D., Irwin, R., Okamura, A.M.: Integration of a particle jamming tactile display with a cable-driven parallel robot. In: Auvray, M., Duriez, C. (eds.) EUROHAPTICS 2014. LNCS, vol. 8619, pp. 258–265. Springer, Heidelberg (2014). https://doi.org/10.1007/978-3-662-44196-1_32

11. Zubrycki, I., Granosik, G.: Novel haptic device using jamming principle for providing kinaesthetic feedback in glove-based control interface. J. Intell. Robot. Syst. Theor. Appl. **85**(3–4), 413–429 (2017)

Musical Applications

Mapping Monophonic MIDI Tracks to Vibrotactile Stimuli Using Tactile Illusions

Byron Remache-Vinueza[1,2](✉) , Andrés Trujillo-León[1,3] ,
Maria-Alena Clim[4] , Fabián Sarmiento-Ortiz[2] , Liliana Topon-Visarrea[2] ,
Alexander Refsum Jensenius[4] , and Fernando Vidal-Verdú[1,3]

[1] Departamento de Electrónica, Universidad de Málaga, 29071 Málaga, Spain
paulremache@uma.es
[2] SISAu Research Group, Facultad de Ingeniería y Tecnologías de la Información y la
Comunicación, Universidad Tecnológica Indoamérica, Quito 170103, Ecuador
[3] Instituto de Investigación Biomédica de Málaga (IBIMA), 29010 Málaga, Spain
[4] RITMO Centre for Interdisciplinary Studies in Rhythm, Time and Motion,
Department of Musicology, University of Oslo, Oslo, Norway

Abstract. In this project, we propose an algorithm to convert musical features and structures extracted from monophonic MIDI files to tactile illusions. Mapping music to vibrotactile stimuli is a challenging process since the perceptible frequency range of the skin is lower than that of the auditory system, which may cause the loss of some musical features. Moreover, current proposed models do not warrant the correspondence between the emotional response to music and the vibrotactile version of it. We propose to use tactile illusions as an additional resource to convey more meaningful vibrotactile stimuli. Tactile illusions enable us to add dynamics to vibrotactile stimuli in the form of movement, changes of direction, and localization. The suggested algorithm converts monophonic MIDI files into arrangements of two tactile illusions: "phantom motion" and "funneling". The validation of the rendered material consisted of presenting the audio rendered from MIDI files to participants and then adding the vibrotactile component to it. The arrangement of tactile illusions was also evaluated alone. Results suggest that the arrangement of tactile illusions evokes more positive emotions than negative ones. This arrangement was also perceived as more agreeable and stimulating than the original audio. Although musical features such as rhythm, tempo, and melody were mostly recognized in the arrangement of tactile illusions, it provoked a different emotional response from that of the original audio.

Keywords: Audio tactile rendering · MIDI · Monophonic music · Tactile illusion · Vibrotactile stimuli

---

Supported by the Spanish Government under contract PID2021-125091OB-I00.

1   Introduction

Experiencing music means more than just perceiving sound. It is a multi-sensory experience as well as a complex cognitive process where tactile and visual modalities play important roles. In fact, musical sound is produced through vibrations may reach our somatosensory system to complement the experience. Recently, researchers have found that it is possible to convert some musical features such as rhythm, frequency, and intensity into tactile stimuli presented to the user through vibrating devices attached to the skin (vibrotactile stimuli) [8]. Different methods have been proposed to convert musical features to perceptible vibrotactile stimuli (see [9] for a review). The strategies used range from complex signal processing to conceptual implementations.

One approach to such mappings consists of placing different frequencies on different parts of the body, the so-called Frequency Model [4]. With this technique, audio signals are processed and separated into different frequency bands to generate sine tones with frequencies found in the skin perception range. Dynamics can be added by extracting the envelope and transients from control signals, which are then arranged in different locations in a music haptic installation that presents vibrotactile stimuli through actuators. The concept of low pitches being "down" and high pitches being "up" is replicated from the bottom to the top of the installation. Even sitting still, participants reported an enhanced feeling of rhythm and sensations of movement [4]. However, researchers agree that some musical information is lost with the Frequency Model when presenting discrete frequencies instead of the whole frequency range of the audio file.

Another method is the Track Model, in which a musical composition is divided into tracks containing different instruments, each routed to different actuators touching the skin. In [5], the effectiveness of the Track Model was evaluated. They report a better performance of the Track Model than the Frequency Model when conveying emotional content, but underline the requirement of multi-track audio files, which are not available for every piece of music.

Moreover, researchers agree that the perceptible frequency range of the skin (3 Hz–1 kHz) is far more limited than that of the auditory system (20 Hz–20 kHz). Therefore, musical information embedded in the higher frequencies is usually lost in the mapping process. In addition, the emotional response to vibrotactile stimuli rendered from musical features remains unclear, thus making it difficult to establish a unified rendering method.

To help overcome these limitations, we explore a resource known as *tactile illusions* (*TIs*) [3,6]. A *TI* may be defined as the discrepancy between a tactile stimulus and what is perceived. What we propose is to use *TIs* to convey more meaningful vibrotactile stimuli. *TIs* enable us to add dynamics; something more than just vibrations, pulses, or beats. *TIs* create sensations of movement, direction, and localization; which are also features used in music [7].

In Sect. 2, the proposed algorithm and the experimental methodology are detailed. In Sect. 3, the results of the main experiments are described. Finally in Sect. 4, the discussion and conclusions are elaborated.

2   Method

2.1   Proposed Algorithm

Audio. Audio was played back from monophonic MIDI files to avoid overlapping notes. One note played at a time is desired since each tactile illusion can be presented just one at a time (i.e., each *TI* corresponds to one note only), see Fig. 3. Musical features derived from the MIDI files are shown in Table 1. Each musical note produces a vector of musical information (i.e., vibrations that can be perceived by the ear using standard audio technology but not easily perceived through touch) as follows: $V_{Ai}(N_i, F_i, t_i, D_i)$.

Table 1. Musical information derived from the MIDI files.

Feature	Representation	Description
Number of notes	n	Total number of notes
Notes	N_i	Note played in position i, with i from 1 to n
Frequency (Hz)	F_i	Frequency of note N_i
Onset time (s)	t_i	Time when note N_i is played
Duration (s)	D_i	How long note N_i is played
Maximum frequency (Hz)	F_{max}	Highest frequency from notes N_1 to N_n
Minimum frequency (Hz)	F_{min}	Lowest frequency from notes N_1 to N_n

Tactile Illusions. The proposed *TIs* to implement are *Phantom Motion* (PM) or *Apparent Movement* [3] and *Funneling* (FUN) or *Illusory Actuator* [6]. These illusions can be created using a pair of actuators similar to stereo headphones. With *PM*, the participant perceives a linear illusory movement of a vibrating point from one actuator to the other, where the frequency of vibrations, duration, and direction of movement can be controlled. *FUN* evokes the sensation of an illusory actuator vibrating in a specified location between the physical actuators, where the frequency of vibrations, duration, and location can also be controlled. Besides the versatility of these illusions, movement of *PM* may be associated with the movement of hands when playing instruments such as violin, piano, or guitar, while *FUN* allows adding dynamics and rhythm when locating short-duration illusory actuators on opposite sides when playing different notes.

Technical and Psychophysical Implications. Technical limitations are especially associated with the design of the actuators. During pilot tests, it was determined that the vibrotactors designed for this project had a satisfactory response 90 Hz and above while overheating was negligible for arrangements with durations of around 60s.

Regarding psychophysical limitations, the skin can perceive vibrations from 3 Hz up to 1 kHz. Therefore, the effective range of frequencies is 90 Hz to 1000 Hz; it means notes from F2# (92.5 Hz) to B5 (987.8 Hz).

Audio–Tactile Mapping. As a first step, MIDI-files with notes out of the effective range are transposed in steps of 1 semitone until F_{max} and F_{min} fall between the allowed range. The direction of transposition depends on the limit that is surpassed. If F_{max} exceeds the upper limit then the transposition is towards a lower tone. On the other hand, if F_{min} is below the lower limit then the transposition is towards a higher tone. If after transposing these frequencies remain out of the effective range, the MIDI file is rejected. The number of notes n from the musical excerpt corresponds to the number of TIs. The fundamental frequency F_i of every note N_i in the MIDI file corresponds to the frequency of vibration of each TI_i. Onset time t_i and duration D_i correspond to the onset time and duration of TI_i, respectively. Depending on the value of D_i, a different TI is selected. In pilot studies, and in [1] and [3], it was found that perceptible PM can be obtained for the whole effective range of frequencies (90 Hz to 1 kHz) and durations from 0.5s up to 2.5s. Longer durations produce an effect of adaptation while shorter ones break the apparent movement into two independent pulses. FUN can be obtained with confidence for the whole effective range of frequencies and durations as low as 0.1s [2]. Although over 2.5s the effect of illusory actuator is weak, it remains perceptible. The composition used to validate this algorithm did not have notes longer than 6.8s. The final conditions are as follow: PM when $0.5s \leq D_i \leq 2.5s$; FUN when $0s < D_i < 0.5s \land D_i > 2.5s$.

The spatial feature SF_i of tactile illusion TI_i (i.e., direction of illusory movement in the case of PM and the location of illusory actuator in the case of FUN) is assigned depending on the direction of the previous TI. If TI PM_{i-1} was from left to right (L-R) then PM_i will be from right to left (R-L), and vice versa. If FUN_{i-1} was on the left side (L) (i.e., between the left actuator and the center) then FUN_i is assigned to the right side (R) (i.e., between the right actuator and the center) and vice versa (See Fig. 2b). If the previous TI was PM_{i-1} from L-R (or R-L) and the following TI is FUN_i, then FUN_i is assigned to the L (or R). Finally, if the previous TI was FUN_{i-1} on the L (or R) and the following TI is PM_i, then PM_i is assigned movement from L-R (or R-L). The initial value SF_1 is assigned randomly.

The final vector in the tactile domain (i.e., vibrations that can be perceived through touch; although some of them may also be audible) is: V_{Ti} (F_i, t_i, D_i, TI_i, SF_i), where TI_i is the TI assigned to note N_i and SF_i is its spatial feature. The flowchart of the algorithm is shown in Fig. 1.

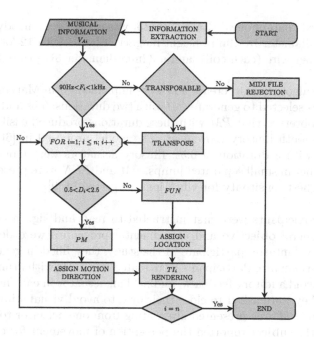

Fig. 1. Flowchart of the proposed algorithm for a MIDI file with n notes (refer to Table 1).

2.2 Experimental Evaluation

To evaluate the effectiveness of the proposed algorithm a randomized, blind, controlled experiment was designed - each participant went through a practice session and then was assigned to either experiment A or B.

Participants. Twenty volunteers from Universidad Tecnológica Indoamérica (students, lecturers, and staff) were recruited; 50% male and 50% female, 19–52 years old ($M = 28.9$, $SD = 9.3$). A total of 70% of the subjects described themselves as music-loving non-musicians, 10% as amateur musicians, other 10% as semiprofessional musicians, and only 1 as non music-loving non-musician. Ten of the participants were randomly assigned to experiment A and the rest to experiment B. All of them took part in a practice session.

Practice Session. The purpose of the practice session was to familiarize the participants with *TIs*. Their recognition is crucial for subjects to be able to evaluate the arrangement of *TIs*.

Apparatus. Two analog outputs of a National Instruments DAQ model USB 6002 were routed to a Fosi Audio stereo amplifier model TDA7498E and then to a pair of voice coil actuators built by the authors based on the design proposed in

[11] and named "hap-phones". Each actuator was made with a neodymium cylindrical 10mm diameter by 10mm height magnet, 4 layers with 12 loops of 0.5mm diameter copper wire (each coil), and a 32mm diameter 3D printed enclosure.

Stimuli. The algorithms to create *TIs* were implemented in Matlab. The model used in [3] was selected to generate *PM* with two durations: 0.5s and 1s. In a pilot study it was observed that *PM* with these durations produced easily perceptible continuous smooth illusory movement. The model proposed in [6] was used to create *FUN* with a duration of 0.5s. Illusory actuators were moving from one side to the other in small separated jumps. *PM* and *FUN* were presented 250 Hz, the skin's highest sensitivity for vibrations suggested in [9].

Procedure Participants were first instructed to read and sign a consent letter where the general objective and experimental procedure were detailed. After accepting to voluntarily participate in the study, they filled in general information in a questionnaire. Participants were seated in a chair with armrests wearing earmuffs to avoid auditory feedback, and held an actuator in each hand as shown in Fig. 2a. They were asked to close their eyes to avoid visual stimuli and favor concentration. *PM* was presented alternating from one actuator to the other in a loop until the subject reported the perception of movement for each duration (i.e., 0.5s and 1s). The participant then evaluated the clarity of the perceived *TI* on a 5-point scale where 0 is imperceptible, 1 almost imperceptible, 2 slightly clear, 3 clear, and 4 very clear. The procedure was replicated for *FUN*.

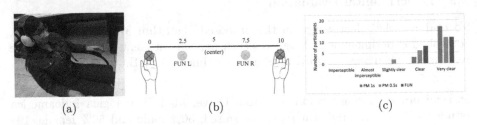

Fig. 2. a) Participant during experimentation, b) Relative locations of illusory actuators for left (2.5) and right(7.5) sides, c) Levels of clarity for *PM* and *FUN*.

The results show that every participant felt both *TIs* (See Fig. 2c). *PM* with both durations was mostly perceived as very clear ($Mo = 4$, $Md = 4$); 17 participants perceived 1s *PM* as very clear and 3 as clear, while 12 participants perceived 0.5s *PM* as very clear, 6 participants as clear, and just 2 as slightly clear. *FUN* was also perceived mostly as very clear ($Mo = 4$, $Md = 4$); 12 participants reported very clear and 8 clear perception of the *TI*. Although changes in the location of the illusory actuator were recognized with ease, their location was not precisely identified. Therefore, only two positions were presented on alternating sides: left and right (explained in Sect. 2.1).

Experimental Session A. The purpose of experiment A was to determine the effect on the emotional response of adding the tactile modality, in the form of a synchronized arrangement of *TIs*, to a musical excerpt.

Apparatus. In addition to the setup used in the practice session, an audio interface Focusrite Scarlett 4i4 was integrated to route the different outputs. Outputs 1 and 2, corresponding to vibrotactile stimuli, were sent to the amplifier and then to the actuators, while outputs 3 and 4, corresponding to audio, were routed to a pair of Sennheiser headphones model HD 240 pro.

Stimuli. The 4th Movement of "mmer" by Vivaldi played by a violin was selected as the musical composition for this experiment. Using the algorithm proposed, an arrangement of *TIs* was obtained. Figure 3 shows eleven seconds of the synchronized session in Audacity. The top stereo channel contains the signals to prompt the *TIs* which are sent to each actuator, while the bottom channel represents the monophonic MIDI file.

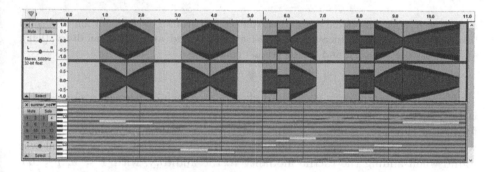

Fig. 3. An 11s excerpt of the MIDI track synchronized with the *TIs*.

Procedure. Participants were instructed to assess the extent to which they felt "Happy", "Sad", "Scary" and "Peaceful" on a scale from 0 absent to 9 present (as done in [10]), as well as the valence and arousal of the excerpt from 0 to 9 (unpleasant-pleasant and relaxing-stimulating, respectively). All participants also reported recognition of musical features: rhythm, tempo, melody, timbre, and genre; a quick and clear description of each feature was presented to avoid confusion. After that, the musical composition synced with the arrangement of *TIs* was presented to the participants, and the evaluation was repeated following the same previous instructions.

Experimental Session B. This experiment aimed to determine the emotional response to the arrangement of *TIs* alone, and to then ascertain any significant difference from the emotional response to the audio excerpt. The apparatus and setup were similar to the practice session. In this experiment, the arrangement of *TIs* was presented without audio.

3 Results

Since a 90% confidence interval overlapped for every emotion, it was not possible to assign a specific emotion to the musical composition [10] - suggesting that the composition elicited blended emotions. Therefore, the statistical analysis focused on each emotion per condition: auditory, auditory-tactile, and tactile (Fig. 4a).

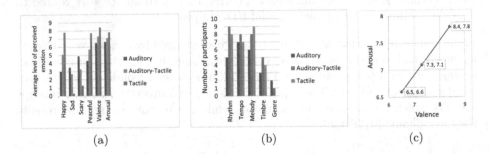

(a)   (b)   (c)

Fig. 4. a) Average emotional evaluation, valence and arousal, b) Recognition of musical features, c) Relation of increase in average valence and arousal for auditory (left), auditory-tactile (center), and tactile (right) conditions.

Using Q-Q graphics it was found that data does not present a normal distribution. Hence, to compare the auditory and auditory-tactile conditions (performed in the same group of participants) a non-parametric Wilcoxon's T-test was used. Only for the emotion labeled as "Happy" a significant increment was found when adding the tactile modality to the auditory, with $T = 0$, $p \leq .05$. For the emotions "Sad", "Scary", and "Peaceful" no significant difference was found ($T = 19$, $p > .05$; $T = 33$, $p > .05$; $T = 6.5$, $p > .05$). Regarding valence and arousal no significant effect was found ($T = 10$, $p > .05$; $T = 11.5$, $p > .05$).

To evaluate the difference between the emotional response for auditory and tactile conditions a non-parametric Mann-Whitney U-test was used. Results show that compared to the auditory condition, the tactile condition was perceived significantly happier and more peaceful ($U = 61$, $p < .05$; $U = 70.5$; $p < .05$), significantly less sad and scary ($U = 134$, $p < .05$; $U = 137$, $p < .05$), and significantly more agreeable and stimulating ($U = 66.5$, $p < .05$; $U = 77$, $p < .05$).

To compare the auditory-tactile and tactile conditions a non-parametric Mann-Whitney U-test was used. The tactile condition was significantly happier than the auditory-tactile ($U = 75$, $p < .05$). For the emotions "Sad", "Scary", and "Peaceful" no significant difference was found ($U = 129$, $p \geq .05$; $U = 130.5$, $p \geq .05$; $U = 80.5$, $p \geq .05$). Regarding valence and arousal, no significant effect was found ($U = 80.5$, $p \geq .05$; $U = 104$, $p \geq .05$). The relation of increase in valence and arousal for auditory, auditory-tactile, and tactile conditions is shown in Fig. 4c.

Rhythm, tempo, and melody were musical features mostly recognized in the auditory-tactile (90%, 80%, 80%, respectively) and tactile (80%, 70%, 90%, respectively) conditions. The less recognized element was genre with 20% for auditory, 10% for auditory-tactile, and 0% for tactile. The best recognized feature in the auditory condition was tempo (70%), in the auditory-tactile condition was rhythm (90%) and in the tactile condition was melody (90%). Overall, musical features were recognized to a grater extent in the auditory-tactile condition, followed by the tactile condition, and finally the auditory condition (see Fig. 4b).

4   Discussion and Conclusions

We have proposed an algorithm to map monophonic MIDI files to arrangements of PM and FUN tactile illusions (TI). Each note of a MIDI file was assigned a TI based on various aspects: onset time, duration, and fundamental frequency. Transposition of notes was required when the maximum and/or minimum frequencies of the musical composition were out of the effective range (90 Hz–1 kHz); a limitation that causes the rejection of some musical compositions. Changes in the direction of PM and the location of FUN were used to control the dynamics of the TIs arrangement. This was supported by a significant increase in perceived arousal when comparing the auditory with the tactile condition. The auditory-tactile condition was found to be "happier" than the auditory condition with no effect identified for valence and arousal. However, the tactile condition presented significant changes in the emotional response compared to the auditory condition as well as in valence and arousal. This was probably because of the novelty of the stimuli and because participants were more focused on the tactile modality (auditory and visual feedback were blocked).

Although the tactile condition was perceived as more positive, it was not possible to assign a specific emotion to any condition, becoming a challenge to define whether the arrangement of TIs evoked similar or different emotional responses. Surprisingly, the arrangement of TIs conveyed rhythm, tempo, and melody to most of the participants and enhanced their perception when presented along with the audio. This suggests that even considering the technical and psychophysical limitations, key elements of music can be embedded into arrangements of TIs. Regardless, experimentation with more participants is required to properly support our suggestions. Currently, we are exploring the emotional response to arrangements of TIs rendered from musical excerpts with tested and confirmed emotional labels (happy, sad, scary, and peaceful) in [10]. In future work we hope to find an algorithm that combines various resources to properly translate music to vibrotactile stimuli.

References

1. Bellicha, A., Trujillo-Leon, A., Bachta, W.: Phantom sensation: when the phantom escapes the bounds of the actuators and the end-point is sensed in the air. In: 2019 IEEE World Haptics Conference (WHC), pp. 91–96. IEEE, July 2019. https://doi.org/10.1109/WHC.2019.8816176, https://ieeexplore.ieee.org/document/8816176/

2. Israr, A., Poupyrev, I.: Tactile brush. In: Proceedings of the SIGCHI Conference on Human Factors in Computing Systems, pp. 2019–2028. ACM, New York, NY, USA, May 2011. https://doi.org/10.1145/1978942.1979235

3. Seo, J., Choi, S.: Initial study for creating linearly moving vibrotactile sensation on mobile device. In: 2010 IEEE Haptics Symposium, pp. 67–70. IEEE, March 2010. https://doi.org/10.1109/HAPTIC.2010.5444677, http://ieeexplore.ieee.org/document/5444677/

4. Karam, M., Russo, F., Branje, C., Fels, D.I.: Towards a model human cochlea: sensory substitution for crossmodal audio-tactile displays. In: Graphics Interface Conference, pp. 267–274 (2008). https://doi.org/10.5555/1375714.1375759

5. Karam, M., Russo, F.A., Fels, D.I.: Designing the model human cochlea: an ambient crossmodal audio-tactile display. IEEE Trans. Haptics 2(3), 160–169 (2009). https://doi.org/10.1109/TOH.2009.32

6. Lee, J., Kim, Y., Jounghyun Kim, G.: Rich pinch: perception of object movement with tactile illusion. IEEE Trans. Haptics 9(1), 80–89 (2016). https://doi.org/10.1109/TOH.2015.2475271, https://ieeexplore.ieee.org/document/7234937/

7. McAngus Todd, N.P.: The kinematics of musical expression. J. Acoust. Soc. Am. 97(3), 1940 (1998). https://doi.org/10.1121/1.412067, https://asa.scitation.org/doi/abs/10.1121/1.412067

8. Merchel, S., Altinsoy, M.E.: Auditory-tactile experience of music. In: Papetti, S., Saitis, C. (eds.) Musical Haptics. SSTHS, pp. 123–148. Springer, Cham (2018). https://doi.org/10.1007/978-3-319-58316-7_7

9. Remache-Vinueza, B., Trujillo-León, A., Zapata, M., Sarmiento-Ortiz, F., Vidal-Verdú, F.: Audio-tactile rendering: a review on technology and methods to convey musical information through the sense of touch. Sensors 21(19), 6575 (2021). https://doi.org/10.3390/S21196575, https://www.mdpi.com/1424-8220/21/19/6575/htmwww.mdpi.com/1424-8220/21/19/6575

10. Vieillard, S., Peretz, I., Gosselin, N., Khalfa, S., Gagnon, L., Bouchard, B.: Happy, sad, scary and peaceful musical excerpts for research on emotions 22(4), 720–752 (2008). https://doi.org/10.1080/02699930701503567, https://www.tandfonline.com/doi/abs/10.1080/02699930701503567

11. Yao, H.Y., Hayward, V.: Design and analysis of a recoil-type vibrotactile transducer. J. Acoust. Soc. Am. 128(2), 619–627 (2010). https://doi.org/10.1121/1.3458852, http://asa.scitation.org/doi/10.1121/1.3458852

Accuracy of Musical Pitch Control Through Finger Pushing and Pulling

Hanna Järveläinen⬤, Stefano Papetti(✉)⬤, and Eric Larrieux⬤

Zurich University of the Arts, Pfingstweidstr. 96, 8005 Zurich, Switzerland
{hanna.jarvelainen,stefano.papetti,eric.larrieux}@zhdk.ch

Abstract. An experiment with trained musicians was conducted to investigate how finger pushing and pulling gestures that control pitch bending of a synthesizer tone affect accuracy with respect to a given target pitch. Additionally, the effect of different interactive vibrotactile feedback was assessed. A self-developed haptic interface called TouchBox was used for this purpose. Finally, subjective evaluations were collected for perceived agency, confidence of correctness, and pleasantness of the experience.

Keywords: Pitch bending · Pitch accuracy · Finger control · Pushing · Pulling · Vibrotactile feedback · User experience

1 Introduction

Novel digital musical interfaces have recently unlocked the possibility to map continuous and multidimensional gestures (e.g. finger pressing, sliding, tapping, etc.) to musical parameters, thus offering enhanced expressivity when controlling synthesizers and virtual instruments [17, 22].

Among the most musically relevant expressive controls, pitch modulation and pitch bending have been traditionally possible to varying degrees on several musical instruments, for instance stringed instruments and even percussion such as the tabla. On those instruments, pitch is typically controlled by deforming the source of vibration (e.g. oscillating or bending the strings or the drum membrane) with the same hand or fingers that play them. Conversely, on electronic and digital instruments – especially keyboard-based ones – pitch-bending is generally delocated and assigned to a spring-loaded lever or wheel, requiring players to dedicate their left hand to operate them. Also, on those devices the speed of pitch modulation is often controlled by a low-frequency oscillator (LFO), while only its amount is controlled in real-time by the player. All that makes the ergonomics of pitch modulation and pitch bending very different on such devices, as compared to traditional musical instruments. Novel digital musical interfaces such as those mentioned above have now reintroduced more natural

This research was pursued as part of project HAPTEEV, funded by the Swiss National Science Foundation (grant 178972).

and direct ways to modulate/bend pitch, for instance by sliding up/down a finger on the same surface that is being played. However, despite the ability to fine tune mapping sensitivity, performing such gesture on digital devices poses a major challenge for control accuracy, possibly also because, unlike traditional instruments, most of them currently do not offer haptic feedback [14].

Young normal-hearing adults reach an auditory pitch discrimination accuracy of 0.5% in a wide frequency range, while musicians can reach even 0.1% [10,19]. Although limited in frequency compared to the audible range, vibrotactile stimuli may also excite a pitch sensation which depends on frequency and amplitude (or energy) [6,20]. Discrimination accuracy between 18% and 3% has been reported [5,15]. Audiotactile interactions exist in perception of consonance, loudness, and pitch through various mechanisms and depending on the task [11,21], but it is unclear if and how a noisy vibrotactile signal might distract auditory pitch control performance, or whether matched auditory and vibrotactile signals might even enhance it.

In the context of musical interfaces, gesture mapping to pitch control, and related open questions concerning audiotactile pitch discrimination, we set out to investigate the action of pitch bending. The pitch of a synthesizer could be bent via pushing forward (pitch up) or pulling backward (pitch down) a finger pressing on top of an interactive surface, until matching a reference pitch. Additionally, two types of vibrotactile feedback were considered, along with a non-vibrating setting.

2   Apparatus

The experiment made use of a self-developed haptic device called TouchBox, which offers a Plexiglas touch panel measuring 3D forces (i.e., along normal, longitudinal and transverse directions), and provides rich vibrotactile feedback. The device is the latest iteration of a former design previously published in open-access form [13].

As shown in Fig. 1, participants sat at a table and pressed a finger on top of the TouchBox, which was placed in front of them. In order to comfortably do so, they could rest their forearm on a support and adjust the height of their seat. A 2 × 2 cm piece of adhesive with fine sandpaper back was stuck at the center of the top panel of the TouchBox, so as to prevent the participants' fingers from slipping while pushing forward or pulling backward.

Auditory feedback, generated by a software synthesizer implemented with Cycling '74 Max, was provided through closed-back headphones (Beyerdynamic DT 770 PRO) connected to a MOTU M4 USB audio interface. The synthesizer reproduced a sawtooth waveform, smoothened by a low-pass filter for a more pleasing sound in view of its prolonged use.

Vibrotactile feedback – also generated in Max in the form of audio signals – was rendered by driving a voice-coil actuator, attached to the bottom of the touch panel, either with the synthesizer's signal or with noise. In the former setting, the goal was to simulate what happens when playing acoustic or electro-acoustic

Fig. 1. The experimental setup.

musical instruments, where the sources of vibration and sound coincide. Since humans are maximally sensitive to vibration in the 200–300 Hz range [20], in order to provide uniformly effective vibrotactile feedback, the sound synthesizer was limited to a pitch range of ± 2 semitones around C4 = 261.6 Hz: therefore the overall range was 233.08–293.66 Hz (B#3-D4). Although narrow, the chosen pitch range did not compromise the pitch matching task, as human frequency discrimination is stable across a wide range 200 Hz to several kHz [3]. For the noise feedback, white noise band-passed in the 40–360 Hz range, again with the goal of maximizing the perceivable feedback, but this time leaving the auditory and tactile channels uncorrelated. Vibration amplitude in both configurations was equalized to 120 dB RMS acceleration (re 10^{-6} m/s^2) so as to be always clearly perceivable [20]. Any sound spillage generated by the actuator was adequately masked by the headphones worn by participants.

A switch pedal, connected via MIDI to the audio interface, allowed participants to record the current pitch of the synthesizer and advance the experiment.

Finally, the table housed a computer screen and a mouse, which were used to give ratings, as described below.

3   Experiment

An experiment was carried out in which the task was to reproduce a target reference pitch as accurately as possible, by controlling a sound synthesizer via the TouchBox.

3.1   Design and Stimuli

The task was carried out under two crossed factors: gesture and vibrotactile feedback. Gesture had two conditions: push forward or pull backward the device's top panel. The two gestures were respectively requested for increasing or decreasing the given initial pitch toward the target. Three vibrotactile feedback conditions were possible: no vibration, noise vibration, and pitched vibration matching the auditory feedback. If vibrotactile feedback was offered in a trial, it was on only while the stimulus (synthesizer sound) was playing.

Target pitches were randomized in a continuous range of ±2 semitones around C4 = 261.6 Hz. Initial pitches of the stimuli were 1 to 3 semitones above or below the target pitch.

Measured variables were: relative pitch accuracy and self-reported ratings on agency ("I felt that I produced the sound"), confidence ("I felt that I gave a correct response"), and pleasantness ("The task felt pleasant").

3.2   Participants and Procedure

Thirty-one normal-hearing, musically trained subjects took part in the experiment (14 F, 17 M, aged 20–39, m = 24.6 years, musical training: m = 16 years). They were trained to execute the task correctly and to use one and same finger of their dominant hand throughout the experiment.

At the beginning of each trial, a target pitch was played back for 3 s. After the reference tone ended, participants adjusted the stimulus pitch to match the target. To minimize confusion and interruptions, trials were organized in two blocks by gesture in random order, and the same vibrotactile feedback was presented in four successive trials. After each block of four trials, ratings on agency, pleasantness, and confidence were collected: participants used the mouse to operate visual analog sliders appearing on the screen, whose values were mapped to the continuous range [0, 1] (0 = very low, 1 = very high).

Total duration of a session, consisting of 72 trials, was roughly 20 min including three short breaks.

4   Results

4.1   Descriptive Analysis

Results are presented in Fig. 2 for the pitch accuracy task and in Fig. 3 for the rating task. These raw data suggest generally larger errors in the pushing gesture. Nevertheless, participants gave consistently higher ratings of agency, confidence, and pleasantness when using the pushing gesture. Notably, participants performed the task somewhat faster with that gesture than with pulling, mean times per trial being 10.6 and 12.0 s, respectively. However, as Fig. 2 shows, participants demonstrate slightly more learning with pushing, as both gestures approach 0.5% accuracy in the last trials, in spite of larger differences between them at the beginning.

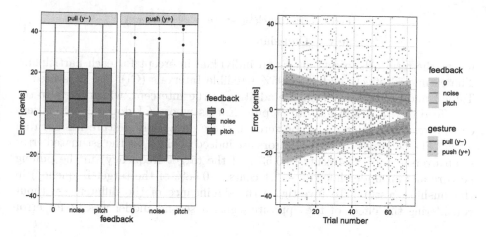

Fig. 2. Left: pitch accuracy (raw data); Right: accuracy as a function of trial number (raw data and linear trend).

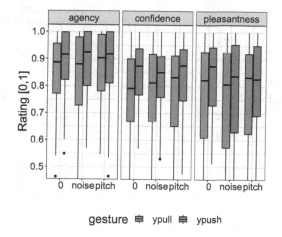

Fig. 3. Evaluation results (raw data).

4.2 Statistical Analysis

Statistical analysis was performed in R using the brms package [1,16]. Statistical models were fit to both accuracy and rating data, and their respective parameters were estimated by Bayesian inference.

Pitch adjustment error (in cents, where cent $= \frac{1}{100}$ of a semitone)[1] was predicted from feedback, gesture, and their interaction. The measured error did not significantly deviate from a normal distribution, so a Gaussian model was fit as follows:

---

[1] The error is computed as $1200 \cdot \log_2(\frac{\text{response frequency}}{\text{target frequency}})$, where 1200 represents an octave range in cents.

$$\text{error} \sim \text{feedback*gesture} + (1|\text{subject})$$
$$\text{family} = \text{Gaussian} \tag{1}$$

where the term (1|subject) allows an individual intercept for each participant. The estimated effects and their 95% Credible Intervals (CI)[2] are presented in Table 1 and Fig. 4. The effects are additive to the Intercept, which refers to the case feedback = 0 and gesture = pull. Effects whose CI do not contain zero can be regarded as credibly non-zero; in these data, only gesture has such an effect. The differences in signed errors are indeed obvious, as the estimated error is an overshoot of 8.74 cents (+0.53% of the target frequency) in the pulling gesture and an undershoot of −12.1 cents (−0.68% of the target frequency) in the pushing gesture. To investigate the significance of the difference without considering the effect of the opposite signs, a second model was fit for error

Table 1. Population-level effects from the statistical model on accuracy (Eq. 1). Estimated effects of conditions are additive to Intercept (feedback = 0, gesture = pull).

	Estimate for error [cents]	Estimation error	l.95..CI	u.95..CI
Intercept	8.73	1.61	5.59	11.83
feedback = noise	0.48	2.03	−3.48	4.47
feedback = pitch	−0.23	2.03	−4.29	3.72
gesture = push	**−20.82**	**2.09**	**−24.94**	**−16.76**
noise:push	−1.22	2.94	−7.04	4.43
pitch:push	0.39	2.97	−5.57	6.29

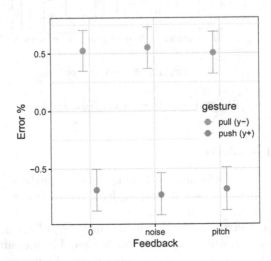

Fig. 4. Estimated effects of feedback and gesture.

---

[2] Credible Interval is the Bayesian 95% confidence interval [7].

values mirrored around zero in the pushing condition. This error estimate was 3.4 cents higher in the pushing gesture, albeit with a 95% CI of $[-0.62, 7.17]$.

Ratings of agency, confidence, and pleasantness were likewise predicted from feedback and gesture using the following statistical model:

$$\text{rating } (\mu) \sim \text{attribute} + \text{feedback} + \text{gesture} + (1|\text{subject})$$
$$\phi \sim 1; \text{ zoi} \sim 1; \text{ coi} \sim 1 \tag{2}$$
$$\text{family} = \text{zero-one inflated beta}$$

The range-limited visual analog scale data deviated from normality, so a zero-one inflated beta (ZOIB) distribution was used [8,9,12]. Four parameters describe the ZOIB distribution: mean (μ) and precision (ϕ) of the beta distribution, the probability of a binary $\{0,1\}$ outcome (zoi), and the conditional probability of outcome $\{1\}$ (coi). In our model (Eq. 2), the mean parameter depends on attribute, feedback, and gesture with an individual intercept for each participant. The other three distribution-specific parameters are modeled with a common intercept only. Based on correlation between the attributes in the raw data, we model them as conditions of the experience ratings and not as separate perceptual dimensions.

Table 2. Population-level effects from the statistical model on attribute ratings (Eq. 2). Parameter estimates are obtained by adding the effects to Intercept (where feedback = 0, gesture = pull, attribute = agency), but effects are modeled on transformed scales (see Sect. 4.2).

	Estimate for rating	Est. Error	l.95..CI	u.95..CI
Intercept	1.55	0.13	1.29	1.80
phi_Intercept	1.90	0.04	1.83	1.97
zoi_Intercept	−1.86	0.07	−2.01	−1.72
coi_Intercept	4.46	0.61	3.41	5.81
feedback = noise	−0.15	0.05	−0.25	−0.05
feedback = pitch	−0.04	0.05	−0.14	0.06
gesture = push	0.22	0.04	0.14	0.31
attribute = confidence	−0.23	0.05	−0.33	−0.12
attribute = pleasantness	−0.42	0.05	−0.52	−0.31

The estimated effects from (Eq. 2) are listed in Table 2. Noise vibration has a credibly negative effect, as do the attributes confidence and pleasantness. Pushing gesture in turn has a credibly positive effect on ratings. In Table 2, the parameter estimates are obtained by adding the effects to the Intercept which refers to the case feedback = 0, gesture = pull, and attribute = agency. Note that the mean parameters are modeled on logit-transformed scales[3], and after adding the values in Table 2 they need to be transformed back to interpret the effects in the original scale. Figure 5 presents the estimated effects transformed back to the slider response scale [0, 1].

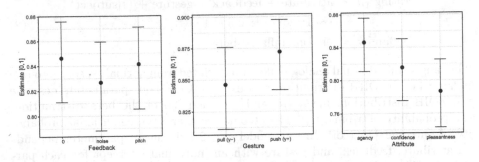

Fig. 5. Estimated conditional effects of feedback, gesture, and attribute on self-reported ratings.

5   Discussion

Average pitch accuracy in the present measurement was roughly 0.6%. This is in line with pitch discrimination thresholds of complex harmonic tones for young normal-hearing adults [10], although musicians can at best reach a 0.1% accuracy [19]. The present ecological conditions should not however be compared to a laboratory setting; our main goal was to investigate effectiveness of common gestures for pitch control.

A general finding was a difference in accuracy between pulling and pushing: pulling (approaching target from a higher pitch) produced on average +0.53% overshoot and pushing (approaching target from a lower pitch) −0.68% undershoot. The data suggest a speed-accuracy trade-off: even though slightly less accurate, pushing took less time and was rated credibly higher in agency, confidence, and pleasantness. Furthermore, mean errors were equalized towards the end of the session, as participants demonstrated slightly more learning in pushing than pulling. All this considered, pushing might be more efficient in tasks that are learned and then performed frequently and require faster execution, such as controlling a musical interface. If the task is new or altogether rare, maximal accuracy seems to be achieved by pulling. In any case, if the gesture is in one direction only, the responses will not quite reach the target from the direction of approach. A combination of both gestures might produce more accurate responses, although for our envisioned musical application this measurement was

---

[3] The logit transformation is given by $x = \log(\frac{p}{1-p})$; its inverse transform is the logistic function $p = \frac{1}{1+e^{-x}}$.

not essential. Of general interest would also be to combine pushing gestures with decreasing pitch and vice versa, in view of the evidence of pitch-verticality and other cross-modal mappings [2,4].

Perhaps surprisingly, vibration had no effect on accuracy. Pitched vibration produced slightly lower errors and noise vibration slightly higher errors than no vibration; however, these effects were not credibly non-zero in the present dataset, and their verification would require a larger-scale experiment. Noise vibration had a credibly negative effect on ratings of agency, confidence, and pleasantness, though. Due to a large number of parameters to be estimated in the ZOIB distribution, there were unfortunately not enough data to include interactions in the statistical model of the experience ratings. The raw data suggest a positive effect of pitched vibrations in the pulling gesture for all three attributes (Fig. 3); this serves as a hypothesis for future experiments.

Our experiment involved musicians only, a choice motivated by our larger goal of integrating haptic and vibrotactile feedback to musical interfaces. Musicians' pitch control skills may have been good enough to allow performing the task with auditory feedback only. It remains to be measured whether early stage learners, children or persons with impaired pitch discrimination could benefit more from vibrotactile feedback, as multisensory enhancement is known to be strongest in conditions where unisensory information is weakly effective [18]. For musicians, this inverse effectiveness might bring benefits in ensemble playing, or when there is background noise.

6 Conclusion

For young adult musicians, pitch control through finger pushing and pulling resulted in the same order of accuracy as that of auditory pitch discrimination experiments in laboratory setting for young normal-hearing adults. There was a slight trade-off between lower errors in pulling, but faster execution and higher ratings of experience in pushing. Synchronized vibrotactile feedback affected subjective ratings but not performance. Overall, our findings may contribute to more efficient design of future gesture-controlled musical interfaces.

Acknowledgements. The authors would like to thank Martin Fröhlich at Zurich University of the Arts for providing the initial hardware and software design of the TouchBox.

References

1. Bürkner, P.C.: brms: an R package for Bayesian multilevel models using Stan. J. Stat. Softw. **80**(1), 1–28 (2017)
2. Casasanto, D., Phillips, W., Boroditsky, L.: Do we think about music in terms of space? Metaphoric representation of musical pitch. In: Proceedings of the Annual Meeting of the Cognitive Science Society (2003)
3. Dai, H., Micheyl, C.: Psychometric functions for pure-tone frequency discrimination. J. Acoust. Soc. Am. **130**(1), 263–272 (2011)

4. Eitan, Z., Timmers, R.: Beethoven's last piano sonata and those who follow crocodiles: cross-domain mappings of auditory pitch in a musical context. Cognition **114**, 405–422 (2010)
5. Franzén, O., Nordmark, J.: Vibrotactile frequency discrimination. Percept. Psychophys. **17**, 480–484 (1975)
6. Harris, J.A., Arabzadeh, E., Fairhall, A.L., Benito, C., Diamond, M.E.: Factors affecting frequency discrimination of vibrotactile stimuli: implications for cortical encoding. PLoS One **1**(1), e100 (2006)
7. Hespanhol, L., Vallio, C.S., Costa, L.M., Saragiotto, B.T.: Understanding and interpreting confidence and credible intervals around effect estimates. Braz. J. Phys. Ther. **23**(4), 290–301 (2019)
8. Kurschke, J.K.: Doing Bayesian Data Analysis - A Tutorial with R, JAGS, and Stan, 2nd edn. Academic Press, Cambridge (2014)
9. Liu, F., Kong, Y.: zoib: an R package for Bayesian inference for beta regression and zero/one inflated beta regression. R J. **7**(2), 34–51 (2015)
10. Moore, B.C.J., Peters, R.W.: Pitch discrimination and phase sensitivity in young and elderly subjects and its relationship to frequency selectivity. J. Acoust. Soc. Am. **91**, 2881 (1992)
11. Okazaki, R., Hachisu, T., Sato, M., Fukushima, S., Hayward, V., Kajimoto, H.: Judged consonance of tactile and auditory frequencies. In: 2013 World Haptics Conference, pp. 663–666 (2013)
12. Ospina, R., Ferrari, S.L.P.: Inflated beta distributions. Stat. Pap. **51**, 111–126 (2010)
13. Papetti, S., Frohlich, M., Schiesser, S.: The TouchBox: an open-source audio-haptic device for finger-based interaction. In: IEEE World Haptics Conference, pp. 491–496 (2019)
14. Papetti, S., Saitis, C.: Musical haptics: introduction. In: Papetti, S., Saitis, C. (eds.) Musical Haptics. SSTHS, pp. 1–7. Springer, Cham (2018). https://doi.org/10.1007/978-3-319-58316-7_1
15. Pongrac, H.: Vibrotactile perception: differential effects of frequency, amplitude, and acceleration. In: 2006 IEEE International Workshop on Haptic Audio Visual Environments and Their Applications (HAVE 2006), pp. 54–59. IEEE (2006)
16. R Core Team: R: A Language and Environment for Statistical Computing. R Foundation for Statistical Computing, Vienna, Austria (2021)
17. Schwarz, D., Liu, W., Bevilacqua, F.: A survey on the use of 2D touch interfaces for musical expression. In: New Interfaces for Musical Expression (NIME), Birmingham, United Kingdom (2020)
18. Spence, C.: Multisensory perception, cognition, and behavior: evaluation the factors modulating multisensory integration. In: Stein, B.E. (ed.) New Handbook of Multisensory Processing. MIT Press (2012)
19. Spiegel, M.F., Watson, C.S.: Performance on frequency-discrimination tasks by musicians and nonmusicians. J. Acoust. Soc. Am. **76**(6), 1690–1695 (1984)
20. Verrillo, R.T.: Vibration sensation in humans. Music Percept. Interdisc. J. **9**(3), 281–302 (1992)
21. Yau, J.M., Weber, A.I., Bensmaia, S.J.: Separate mechanisms for audio-tactile pitch and loudness interactions. Front. Psychol. **1**, 160 (2010)
22. Zappi, V., McPherson, A.P.: Dimensionality and appropriation in digital musical instrument design. In: 14th International Conference on New Interfaces for Musical Expression, NIME 2014, London, United Kingdom, 30 June–4 July 2014, pp. 455–460 (2014)

Perception of Guitar Strings on a Flat Visuo-Haptic Display

Baptiste Rohou-Claquin[1]([✉]), Malika Auvray[1], Jean-Loïc Le Carrou[2], and David Gueorguiev[1]

[1] Sorbonne Université, CNRS, Institut des Systèmes Intelligents et de Robotique, 4 Place Jussieu, 75005 Paris, France
rohouclaquin@isir.upmc.fr
[2] Sorbonne Université, CNRS, Institut Jean Le Rond d'Alembert, équipe LAM, 4 Place Jussieu, 75005 Paris, France

Abstract. There is a rapid growth of interest in digital musical instruments due to advantages they present over their physical counterparts such as portability and novel experiences. However, these instruments still rarely provide haptic feedback, which results in weakened user experience. This study investigates whether haptic renderings of three guitar strings are discriminated by touch and whether they provide a realistic sensation of plucking a guitar string. Specifically, five methods to record and replay the vibrations induced by the plucking of a guitar string were tested. Three procedures relied on recordings made on the right hand's index finger, which underwent three types of filtering. Another one was recorded on the left hand kept motionless on the guitar's fingerboard. The fifth method recorded the vibrations directly on the neck of the guitar. The results revealed that good discrimination of the rendered string occurred only for recordings made on the motionless left hand's index finger or on the guitar. Participants also rated these conditions as being the most realistic, regardless of whether they were acquainted with musical instruments. Overall, this study shows that distinct guitar strings can be rendered by vibrotactile feedback and that tactile noise due to the interaction impairs their recognition and perceived realism.

Keywords: Vibrotactile rendering · Guitar string discrimination · Visuo-haptic perception

1 Introduction

The field of musical instruments becomes increasingly digitalized, creating a category of instruments called digital musical instruments (DMI). This new category of instruments brings several advantages in comparison to their physical counterparts by overcoming the physical limitations imposed on tangible instruments [17]. However, despite these advantages [6, 16], DMIs currently suffer from

Supported by UFR d'Ingénierie de Sorbonne Université and ANR Maptics.

a large drawback compared to real instruments, which is the absence of haptic feedback. When a musician plays an instrument, a loop is created in the sense of touch. The musician gives energy and perceives the instrument's response, creating a rich haptic exchange. The absence of compelling haptic feedback does not allow for this loop to be obtained in an optimal manner, thus diminishing the musician's ability to control the device and express itself. In addition, the performance and fidelity of the notes are reduced, and the listeners are also impacted by a less expressive performance [14]. Indeed, the sense of touch is an essential sense for interacting with world around us. It enables us to explore the surrounding environment [10] and exhibits an astonishing sensitivity to subtle vibrations up to 1000 Hz [3] as well as small transient changes in the contact forces [7].

Various studies have already investigated the impact of adding a haptic feedback on musical instruments [1,11,15,20] and conclude that such feedback can be helpful for musical perception. The addition of a haptic feedback is useful to improve the quality of play of the musician, but also, it increases the ease of learning, and the pleasure of practicing. Moreover, it facilitates access to people suffering from visual, auditory or deaf blindness impairments [12,18,19]. In order to feel these digital instruments, it is necessary to be able to perceive their textures and vibrations and numerous studies have shown that it is possible to discriminate textures, edges, shapes or vibrations that are generated by haptic devices [2,5,8]. Moreover, coupling haptic feedback with visual representation improves perceptual capacity [9,13], representation in memory [4], and spatio-temporal accuracy [1]. This study aims to investigate how different types of haptic rendering of a guitar string, which are coupled with an accurate visual rendering, are discriminated and perceived by users. Specifically, we investigate the capacity of users to recognize each digital string and their rating of the achieved realism in five experimental conditions.

2   Materials and Methods

2.1   Data Collection

To be able to compare different methods for haptic rendering of guitar string's vibrations, we measured the vibrations elicited by the string on different locations:

- The tip of the right hand's index finger: The measure is performed while this hand plucks the string (Fig. 1.A).
- The tip of the left hand's index finger: This finger pushes on the string at the level of the guitar's fingerboard and stays motionless during the recording (Fig. 1.B).
- The guitar fingerboard: The measure was performed with the accelerometer placed directly on the wood of the guitar's neck (Fig. 1.C).

These measuring locations aimed to test whether signal components generated during the movement or during the interaction between the sensor and the nail impact the discrimination capacity of the user and the sensation of realism. The guitar was held in a natural way; the right hand plucks the string, the left hand holds the neck and pushes on the string. The measures were performed with a PCB352A21 accelerometer that has a sensitivity of 10 mV/g, a measure range of ± 500 g pk, and a frequency range between 1.0 10000 Hz. The data were collected with a sampling frequency of 6250 Hz. For each position, three different notes were recorded corresponding to the vibration of three open strings: High (note E_4) 329 Hz, Medium (note G_3) 196 Hz and Low (note A_2) 110 Hz. These three open strings were found sufficiently spaced in frequency to enable recognition significantly above chance but still challenging enough to prevent perfect performance.

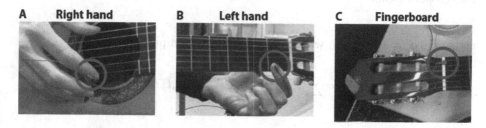

Fig. 1. Measurement of the string's vibration with an accelerometer placed at several locations. A) On the right hand's index finger. B) On the left hand's index finger. C) On the guitar fingerboard

2.2 Spectral Analysis

After collecting the data, the frequency spectrum of each recording was characterized through a fast Fourier transform. The frequency spectra recorded on the right hand (Fig. 2.A) and on the left hand (Fig. 2.B) differ mostly by the presence of low frequency distortion related to the plucking of the strings by the right hand. In the case of measurements performed directly on the guitar fingerboard (Fig. 2.C), the transmitted frequencies are less attenuated than in the other two cases where they are filtered by the skin.

Out of the recordings on the right hand's index finger, we generated three haptic signals: the original signal (Right hand), a low-pass filtered version 70 Hz (Right hand < 70 Hz), a high-pass filtered version 70 Hz (Right hand > 70 Hz). We implemented these frequency filters to preferentially activate the tactile channels respectively related to FA1 (<70 Hz) and FA2 (>70 Hz) tactile afferents with the aim to investigate whether filtering low-frequency tactile noise or the high-frequency peaks would impact perception.

2.3 Visual Interface

In addition to the haptic feedback, a visual feedback of the strings' vibration was implemented on Java Processing (Fig. 3) following the equation of a vibrating

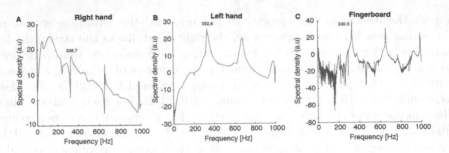

Fig. 2. Fast Fourier transform of the guitar string vibration signals, which are measured with the accelerometer. A) Right hand's signal. B) Left hand's signal. C) Guitar fingerboard's signal.

string fixed at both ends, which was analytically computed:

$$y(x,t) = \sum_{p=1}^{N} A(p) \sin\left(\frac{p\pi}{L}x\right) \cos\left(\omega_p t\right) e^{-0.1\omega_p t} \tag{1}$$

With:

$$\omega_p = \frac{p\pi}{L}\sqrt{\frac{T}{\mu}} \tag{2}$$

$$A(p) = \frac{2a}{p^2\pi^2}\frac{1}{\alpha(1-\alpha)}\sin\left(p\pi\alpha\right) \tag{3}$$

For each note, Eq. 1 was implemented in real time, except for a slight delay generated by the software ($\simeq 2\,$ms). A represents the amplitude of the string in relation to the y-axis (width of the screen), α represents the ratio of the location where the string is plucked in comparison to the total length. Several mechanical parameters related to the string are also considered. L represents the total length of the string, T is the string tension, ω_p is the angular frequency, which coincides with the harmonic frequency (f_p), and μ represents its linear mass. There are also some parameters specific to the simulation such as the sampling frequency, the harmonic number p, and the total number of harmonics N. We computed only the fundamental frequency for the visual rendering because we were limited by the refresh rate of the visual display (p = 1, N = 1, High = 329 Hz, Medium = 196 Hz and Low = 110 Hz).

2.4   Perception Study

To conduct the perception study, a vibrotactile actuator MM3C (Tactile Labs, Canada) was used. This actuator is specially designed to cover the frequency range perceived by the human finger. However, it distorts the signal at very low frequencies (<30 Hz). In order to minimize disturbance during the test, a high-pass finite impulse response filter (FIR) 30 Hz was used on each sample. No

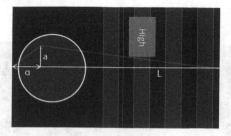

Fig. 3. Representation of a guitar string on the visuo-haptic display.

other distortion was observed during reproduction of the signals hence we did not apply additional low-pass filtering. In addition to the actuator, a 7-in. touch screen was used with a display frequency 47 Hz. It enabled the participants to physically pluck the string, thus adding realism to the action.

Participants had to recognize three types of notes: high (E_4), medium (G_3) and low (A_2). For each of the five types of feedback, a total of 30 samples had to be recognized (10 per note type). The users place the index finger of their non-dominant hand on the actuator, which is located at the top of the screen (Fig. 4). Then, they pluck the string on the tablet with their dominant hand, as if they were playing on a real guitar (Fig. 4). After releasing the string, visual and haptic feedbacks are played simultaneously. Finally, after a few seconds, another screen appears that asks the participants which note was played: high, medium, or low. They choose one of them by pressing the corresponding button. The order of the blocks and of the notes within them are pseudo-randomized. In addition to recognizing the notes, participants are asked to rate the realism of the feedback they had just played in comparison with the impression of playing with a physical guitar. The score is reported using a scroll bar between 0 and 100%. Before each experimental block, which relates to a specific feedback type, participants familiarize themselves with the feedback by playing each note twice with knowledge of its type.

This study took place in an isolated space and participants wore ear muffs and earplugs in order to prevent auditory feedback. The study lasted between 25 and 30 min. In total, 21 people participated, 7 women and 14 men (mean age = 31.2, SD = 11.8). Participants also answered a questionnaire about their musical knowledge and experience with guitar playing. They rated their level of musical knowledge on a Likert-scale from 1 to 7 and they additionally reported whether it relates to guitar. 11 participants self-reported as guitarists among the 21 of the study. This question aimed to probe whether their musical knowledge influences their answers to the task. This study was conducted in accordance with the principles of the declaration of Helsinki and all participants gave their informed consent.

 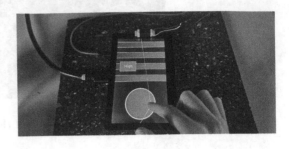

Fig. 4. The experimental set-up and the user's interaction with the simulated string

3   Results

To investigate the impact of the feedback type on recognition of the played note and the sensation of realism, we performed one-way ANOVA statistical analyses after verification of the data by a d'Agostino-Pearson normality test. The ANOVA analysis related to recognition of high, medium, and low notes between the five feedbacks (Fig. 5.A) showed a significant effect of the haptic feedback type on the capacity of discrimination ($F = 8.713$, $p = 0.0002$). A post-hoc Tukey's multiple comparisons test was performed between individual feedbacks. Five post-hoc comparisons were found significant with $p < 0.05$: right hand vs. fingerboard, right hand < 70 Hz vs. left hand, right hand < 70 Hz vs. fingerboard, right hand > 70 Hz vs. left hand, and right hand > 70 Hz vs. fingerboard. Overall, significant comparisons occurred only between the feedbacks related to the right hand's recordings and those related to the left hand or fingerboard recordings.

Another ANOVA was performed on the ratings about the feedback realism (Fig. 5.B). The results from the analyses showed a significant effect of the feedback type on the quality of the rating ($F = 7.444$, $p = 0.0002$). Five post-hoc comparisons were also found significant with $p < 0.05$: right hand vs. left hand, right hand vs. fingerboard, right hand < 70 Hz vs. fingerboard, right hand > 70 Hz vs. left hand, and right hand > 70 Hz vs. fingerboard. Overall, the significant differences observed for the recognition task were similar to those observed for rating the realism.

Generally, it appears that haptic feedback generated from recordings on the right hand, which is plucking the string, are less recognized and appreciated compared to the other feedback types.

The statistical test did not show significant differences between the experimental conditions related to the right hand either for note recognition or realism rating. Thus, filtering the signal recorded on the hand that plucks the guitar did not impact perception. The confusion matrices of the three main feedbacks were also computed showing similar trends. The confusion matrix when the feedback

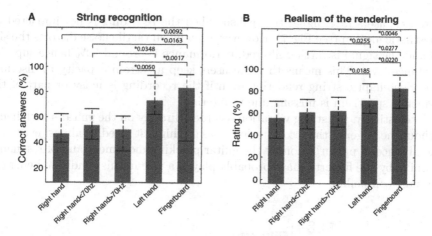

Fig. 5. A) Percentage of correct answers at the recognition task. The blue bars represent the median across participants and the error bars represent the lower and upper quartiles. B) Same plot for the rating of realism. (Color figure online)

stems from recordings on the right hand (Fig. 6.A) has a success rate of about 50%, unlike the other two matrices that have success rates over 70% (Fig. 6.B & C). They also show that confusion mainly occurs between the high and medium notes, whose recognition is worse than for the low note regardless of the feedback type.

A	Right hand			B	Left hand			C	Fingerboard		
	High	Med	Low		High	Med	Low		High	Med	Low
High	50	31.43	10	High	74.29	29.52	8.10	High	67.62	35.24	0.95
Med	32.86	53.33	33.33	Med	18.57	62.86	8.10	Med	27.62	60.95	9.52
Low	17.14	15.24	56.67	Low	7.14	7.62	83.81	Low	4.76	3.81	89.52

Fig. 6. Confusion matrix of the users' correct answers for the different feedback types. A) The right hand's feedback without filtering. B) The left hand's feedback. C) The guitar fingerboard's feedback

4 Discussion

The results of our study show that haptic feedback that stem from recordings on the hand that is plucking the string is significantly less recognized and appreciated than when the feedback is recorded on the immobile left hand's index finger or on the guitar itself. Thus, the tactile noise generated by the kinesthetic interaction has a real impact on discrimination capacity, strongly reducing it.

Moreover, users rate higher the realism when the recording is not impacted by kinesthetic motion (see Fig. 7). However, even when tactile noise distorts the signal and the signal is further filtered, performance is around 50% hence superior to chance level. This means that the users keep a certain capacity to discriminate visuo-haptic string rendering even if the recording is noisy or part of the frequency spectrum is missing due to filtering.

Interestingly, the string vibration recorded directly on the guitar's neck hence without the finger in the recording loop was the highest rated by almost everyone. The absence of perturbation by the guitar plucking movement and of resonance damping by the fingertip have probably played a role in this condition being felt the most compelling.

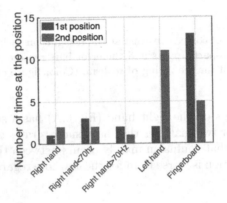

Fig. 7. User preferences. In blue, the feedbacks that obtained the highest ratings by the users during the experiment. In orange, those whose rating was the 2nd highest. (Color figure online)

We can make a slight reservation concerning the similarities in the discrimination and rating abilities of the users between the three conditions that were designed by filtering the measurements on the right hand. The objective of the filtering differentiating the three feedbacks was to target the activation frequencies of the tactile channels related to FA1 and FA2 tactile afferents, respectively. However, the resulting signals still encompassed tactile noise around the cut-off frequency, which blurred the differences between the three conditions that used the recording from the right hand.

However, this does not affect the conclusion that the feedbacks, in which tactile noise due to kinesthetic interaction is present, are significantly less recognized and are rated as less realistic. In spite of the fact that presentation of the experimental blocks (i.e. feedback types) and the order of the trials were randomized between participants, we still noticed a learning phenomenon during the experiment (Fig. 8). The recognition performance continuously improves with the progression of the blocks (Pearson's Correlation, $p = 0.0193$). This progression may be due at first to the discovery of the experiment, which might have required some time to master. However, it is astonishing that performance at recognizing the notes continued to improve after the first blocks had passed.

We also asked participants to rate their musical knowledge and whether it relates to guitar. However, we found no indication that musical experience or experience with guitar playing influenced their perception of the rendered guitar strings.

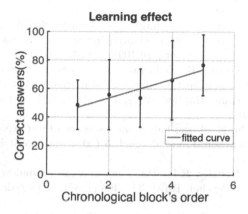

Fig. 8. A linear fit is performed on the average of individual performances across the experimental blocks in chronological order (Mean ± SD).

5   Conclusion

Our study shows that recognition of a digital guitar string varies greatly depending on how the signal is recorded. Users perform better with feedback without the tactile components related to string plucking, thus when sensing solely the instrument's response. Furthermore, the realism of string vibrations recorded on the motionless finger or directly on the guitar is consistently rated higher by participants with a further preference for the direct recording on the guitar.

References

1. Altinsoy, M.E., Merchel, S.: Touchscreens and musical interaction. In: Papetti, S., Saitis, C. (eds.) Musical Haptics. SSTHS, pp. 239–255. Springer, Cham (2018). https://doi.org/10.1007/978-3-319-58316-7_12
2. Bau, O., Poupyrev, I., Israr, A., Harrison, C.: TeslaTouch: electrovibration for touch surfaces, pp. 283–292 (2010). https://doi.org/10.1145/1866029.1866074
3. Bolanowski, S.J., Gescheider, G.A., Verrillo, R.T., Checkosky, C.M.: Four channels mediate the mechanical aspects of touch. J. Acoust. Soc. Am. **84**(5), 1680–1694 (1988). https://doi.org/10.1121/1.397184

4. Ernst, M., Bülthoff, H.: Merging the senses into a robust percept. Trends Cogn. Sci. **8**, 162–9 (2004). https://doi.org/10.1016/j.tics.2004.02.002
5. Fiedler, T., Vardar, Y.: A novel texture rendering approach for electrostatic displays. In: International Workshop on Haptic and Audio Interaction Design - HAID2019, Lille, France, March 2019. https://hal.archives-ouvertes.fr/hal-02011782
6. Frid, E.: Accessible digital musical instruments-a review of musical interfaces in inclusive music practice. Multimodal Technol. Interact. **3**(3) (2019). https://doi.org/10.3390/mti3030057
7. Gueorguiev, D., Vezzoli, E., Mouraux, A., Lemaire-Semail, B., Thonnard, J.L.: The tactile perception of transient changes in friction. J. R. Soc. Interface **14**(137), 20170641 (2017). https://doi.org/10.1098/rsif.2017.0641
8. Gueorguiev, D., Vezzoli, E., Sednaoui, T., Grisoni, L., Lemaire-Semail, B.: The perception of ultrasonic square reductions of friction with variable sharpness and duration. IEEE Trans. Haptics **12**(2), 179–188 (2019). https://doi.org/10.1109/TOH.2019.2894412
9. Lacey, S., Sathian, K.: Visuo-haptic multisensory object recognition, categorization, and representation. Front. Psychol. **5** (2014). https://doi.org/10.3389/fpsyg.2014.00730
10. Lederman, S.J., Klatzky, R.L.: Hand movements: a window into haptic object recognition. Cogn. Psychol. **19**(3), 342–368 (1987). https://doi.org/10.1016/0010-0285(87)90008-9
11. Merchel, S., Altinsoy, E., Stamm, M.: Tactile music instrument recognition for audio mixers. J. Audio Eng. Soc. (8142) (2010). http://www.aes.org/e-lib/browse.cfm?elib=15438
12. Nanayakkara, S.C., Wyse, L., Ong, S.H., Taylor, E.A.: Enhancing musical experience for the hearing-impaired using visual and haptic displays. Hum. Comput. Interact. **28**(2), 115–160 (2013). https://doi.org/10.1080/07370024.2012.697006
13. Newell, F.N.: Visuo-haptic perception of objects and scenes. In: Kaiser, J., Naumer, M. (eds.) Multisensory Object Perception in the Primate Brain, pp. 251–271. Springer, New York (2010). https://doi.org/10.1007/978-1-4419-5615-6_14
14. Papetti, S., Saitis, C. (eds.): Musical Haptics. SSTHS, Springer, Cham (2018). https://doi.org/10.1007/978-3-319-58316-7
15. Passalenti, A., et al.: No strings attached: force and vibrotactile feedback in a virtual guitar simulation. In: 2019 IEEE Conference on Virtual Reality and 3D User Interfaces (VR), pp. 1116–1117 (2019). https://doi.org/10.1109/VR.2019.8798168
16. Serafin, S., Erkut, C., Kojs, J., Nilsson, N., Nordahl, R.: Virtual reality musical instruments: state of the art, design principles, and future directions. Comput. Music. J. **40**(3), 22–40 (2016). https://doi.org/10.1162/COMJ_a_00372
17. Smith, J.O.: Physical Audio Signal Processing. W3K Publishing (2010). http://ccrma.stanford.edu/~jos/pasp/. Online book
18. Trivedi, U., Alqasemi, R., Dubey, R.: Wearable musical haptic sleeves for people with hearing impairment. In: Proceedings of the 12th ACM International Conference on Pervasive Technologies Related to Assistive Environments, PETRA 2019, pp. 146–151. Association for Computing Machinery, New York (2019). https://doi.org/10.1145/3316782.3316796

19. Turchet, L., Baker, D., Stockman, T.: Musical haptic wearables for synchronisation of visually-impaired performers: a co-design approach. In: ACM International Conference on Interactive Media Experiences, IMX 2021, pp. 20–27. Association for Computing Machinery, New York (2021). https://doi.org/10.1145/3452918.3458803
20. Turchet, L., West, T., Wanderley, M.M.: Touching the audience: musical haptic wearables for augmented and participatory live music performances. Pers. Ubiquit. Comput. **25**(4), 749–769 (2020). https://doi.org/10.1007/s00779-020-01395-2

Author Index

Printed in the United States
by Baker & Taylor Publisher Services